GONE NORTH

Welshmen in Rugby League
Volume II

ROBERT GATE

PUBLISHED BY R. E. Gate, Mount Pleasant Cottage,
Ripponden Bank, Ripponden,
Sowerby Bridge, HX6 4JL

ISBN 0 9511190 3 6

Printed and Bound
Joseph Ward Ltd.,
The Ring Road,
Wellington Road
Dewsbury, W. Yorks.

For Bill, "me dad"

Billy O'Neill. Top line-out man for Cardiff and Wales R.U.
Signed for Warrington in 1908.

Contents

Stuart Llewellyn, scorer of over 200 tries for St. Helens,
in action at Wembley, 1953.

Acknowledgements

I owe thanks to the following people who have loaned photographic material, supplied or verified facts and figures or generally assisted in the production of this volume:

Timothy Auty
Malcolm Bentley
Stuart Berry
James Carter
Ken Dalby
Ernie Day
Trevor Delaney ("Code 13")
Harry Edgar ("Open Rugby")
John Edwards
David Howes
Michael Latham
Tony Lewis

Graham Morris
Paul Ogden
Garfield Owen
Chris Park
"The Rugby Leaguer"
Irvin Saxton (RL Record Keepers Club)
The Late Joe Thompson
David Thorpe
The late Tom Webb
Nigel Williams
Nigel Winnard

Frank Wilson (ex-Cardiff R.U.), one of 16 Welshmen to have scored 200 tries in Rugby League.

(*Courtesy "The Rugby Leaguer"*)

Foreword

At the time Volume I of "Gone North" was published (1986) the Welsh connection with Rugby League was almost severed for the first time since the Northern Union sprang into life in 1895. A mere handful of Welshmen were on the books of the professional clubs although BARLA was gaining some ground in South Wales. Cardiff City Blue Dragons had metamorphosed into Bridgend Blue Dragons and finally died the death the pessimists had predicted and probably longed for. Welsh Rugby Union seemed incapable any longer of producing the talent to whet the appetites of discerning Rugby League clubs, who, anyway, could get much better value from BARLA products or from ready-made Australian or New Zealand League players.

Perhaps not too much has changed in the meantime. True, there has been a mini-exodus of Welsh players to League. Welsh caps Terry Holmes, who proved that he "had it" but came too late and ultimately too fragile, Gary Pearce, Rob Ackerman and Stuart Evans have all trekked north and it would now be possible to field a Welsh XIII of sorts – just. On the amateur Rugby League front Wales remains as tough a nut as ever to crack and progress moves at a snail's pace.

Yet the past couple of years have seen Rugby League and Welsh Rugby Union locked together in the head-lines at regular intervals. The protracted Steve Ford affair served to high-light surely the most elastic laws in Creation, the laws pertaining to amateurism in rugby, as perceived by the Rugby Union powers-that-be. Of course, Ford was naive in the extreme to think that he could actually trial (allegedly without payment) for a professional League club, announce that he had signed and then change his mind and expect to be allowed to play Union again. The Welsh Rugby Union, probably mindful of the many more celebrated players currently in its ranks who had also trialled but remained silent and therefore pristine amateur, admitted that Ford was unlucky but could do nothing about reinstating him, his error not having been to commit the crime but to have been caught!

Just how the Rugby Union legislators could square the Ford affair with Naas Botha's flirtation with American Football, hardly the last bastion of the Corinthian ethic, Jonathan Davies' and David Bishop's auctioneering acts and "rebel" tours to South Africa, are feats of judgemental contortionism that beggar description.

Of course, it would be as ingenuous as Steve Ford's expectation of reinstatement to believe that the Rugby Union authorities will ever come clean on their own laws relating to professionalism. After all, the Five Nations Championship would be reduced to three and there would be no more tours from or to Australia, New Zealand or South Africa, and even fewer Welshmen would turn to League!

In the meantime, captive reader, regale yourselves with memories of the genii Wales used to produce and export to a welcoming and appreciative northland.

Ripponden   ROBERT GATE
February, 1988

Chapter 1

Ben Gronow
(Bridgend RU, Huddersfield NU, Batley RL and Featherstone Rovers RL)

and

Johnny Rogers
(Bridgend RU, Cardiff RU, Huddersfield NU, Wakefield Trinity RL)

Bridgend, a small, unremarkable township on the banks of the River Ogwr some sixteen miles to the west of Cardiff, has spawned a myriad gifted rugby footballers – around two dozen have attained Welsh International status, some of whom were giants of the Union game. Men such as Bobby Delahay, Vivian Jenkins, Roddy Evans, John Lloyd and J.P.R. Williams have created their own legends under the amateur laws. Other caps from Bridgend such as Billy Moore, Dan Pascoe, Ken Richards and latterly Steve Fenwick successfully transferred their skills to the professional code.

The two sons of Bridgend featured here experienced closely interwoven careers which reached a zenith in the years immediately prior to and following the Great War when they were members of the team of all teams, Harold Wagstaff's Huddersfield. Enshrined in Rugby League lore as "The Team of All the Talents", the men who donned the famous claret and gold hoops of the Fartown club swept all before them in an orgy of trophy taking and record breaking. Between 1911 and 1922 Wagstaff's wonders annexed no fewer than seventeen major trophies. In a team overflowing with star performers Johnny Rogers and Ben Gronow were not outshone.

Ben was born in Bridgend on March 3rd, 1887, five years before Rogers, christened John Henry, first saw the light of day in nearby Tondu. Growing up among six brothers and two sisters in Bridgend Ben Gronow found out early in life that rugby football was to be his calling. He was rugby-mad – the thing to be in Bridgend. From street rugby Ben followed the well-worn path through Bridgend Harlequins and on to senior football with Bridgend at the tender age of sixteen. He had commenced his career as a full-back, where his wonderful kicking powers indicated his place should be, but soon graduated to the forwards.

It is doubtful whether the old Quarella ground was ever graced by a finer forward than Gronow. By 1908-09 he had risen to the club

Ben Gronow

captaincy and had made the first of his sixteen appearances with Glamorganshire. The following season saw him win a place in all four of Wales' International matches. New Year's Day, 1910 was the occasion of his Welsh debut as France were dispatched 49-14 at Swansea with the young Gronow scoring a try. A fortnight later Wales met England in the first International match to be staged at Twickenham and Ben earned his everlasting place in Rugby Union history by kicking off on that momentous occasion. He would not have been amused however by the result of his kick for the passage of play that followed led to England's winger Chapman scoring a try within a minute of the start. In the pack with Ben that day were Joe Pugsley of Cardiff and Jim Webb of Abertillery who later went north to Salford and St. Helens respectively. The Welsh lost to the English (6-11) for the first time since 1898 but Ben shared in wins against Scotland (14-0) in a quagmire at Cardiff and against Ireland (19-3) in Dublin.

Ben's sterling displays had been noted by the eagle-eyed Northern Union scouts but it was Ebbw Vale NU club which first approached him to turn professional. Their offer of £25 and a job (he was apprenticed to a mason at the time) was not enough to tempt him however and it was Huddersfield who obtained his signature on May 14th, 1910 for the not inconsiderable sum of £120.

As coincidence would have it, Gronow's debut for Huddersfield was against Ebbw Vale at Fartown on September 3rd, 1910, a game won by 21-3. Ben was not an immediate success, probably because he was trying to disguise a thigh strain which he had picked up in a practice match in August. After appearing in an 11-2 defeat at Headingley in his second match he was demoted to the reserves to learn the complexities of the game. He learnt quickly and by the end of his first season had made 31 appearances in the first team, had won a Welsh cap against England at Coventry on 12th December and had gained his first medal, albeit a runners-up, by appearing in the Yorkshire Cup Final against Wakefield Trinity who defeated the Fartowners 8-2 at Leeds.

A corner-stone of Huddersfield's mighty, mobile and talented pack, Ben Gronow cut a dashing figure. A powerful physique was one of his main attributes as he stood a shade over six feet tall and at his peak weighed over sixteen stones. He wore size ten boots but never seemed to be able to squeeze into his jersey which was always "fit to bust" on his huge frame. He had huge hands and elongated arms which enabled him to suddenly fire out long, telling passes from seemingly impossible positions to set up unexpected passing movements. His dark brooding countenance belied his passion for action on the football field and it was a brave man who fell at his feet when he decided to dribble the oval, an art which was one of his specialities. For his own part he was a master at stopping foot-rushes and his tackling was of a high order. Like his fellow packman, the great Douglas Clark, a world champion wrestler, Ben had

Johnny Rogers

the ability to force his victim to go just where he wanted him to go and those long arms soon saw to it that the poor fellow got no further.

Although he was an exceptional forward *per se* it was as a kicker of goals that Ben Gronow was most renowned. In his first four seasons at Fartown Gronow kicked only 20 goals as Huddersfield preferred to employ the talents of half-back Tommy Grey, full-back Major Holland or centre Edgar Wrigley. Even Johnny Rogers had taken precedence over Ben in the goal-kicking stakes in 1913-14, a season in which Holland set up a new record for the Northern Union by landing 131 goals. Included among these were eighteen kicked in a first round Challenge Cup-tie against Swinton Park which Huddersfield won by 119-2 (Feb 28th, 1914). This remains the highest score recorded in a first-class RL match. Australian three-quarters Rosenfeld and Gleeson scored seven and five tries respectively and there were a couple each for Gronow and Rogers, who also contrived to kick a goal.

It was not until a game at Bramley on December 5th, 1914 that Gronow became Fartown's regular marksman. In a 34-7 victory Ben had eight shots at goal and hit the target every time. He now began to make up for lost time and the following week at Fartown kicked nine goals in a 60-7 win over Bradford Northern. On January 30th, 1915 he put eleven goals over the bar in a 79-0 rout of poor old Bramley and on April 5th he had ten goals to his credit as Barrow went down 59-5. By the end of the season Major Holland's record had been eclipsed as Ben rattled up 140 goals. He had also created a record number of points by claiming 292 to pass by 12 Jim Lomas' total set in 1906-07. In the first full season after the war (1919-20) Gronow extended both records by kicking 148 goals and amassing 332 points although both would soon fall to an even greater goal-kicking Welshman, Jim Sullivan, who set new marks in 1922-23.

Ben kicked over 800 goals in his career but how many more might he have scored had his talent been recognised four years earlier and had not the Kaiser's War interrupted peaceful pursuits such as rugby football? Down the years there have been many wonderful goal-kickers but not many performed the duty with so little fuss and consummate ease as the burly Fartowner. Having aligned the ball to his satisfaction he took a run without any mannerism, swung his mighty right boot and followed through in the best text-book style. There was an air of inevitability about his kicking.

The story of Ben Gronow's first connection with Johnny Rogers is related in the benefit brochure for Ben published in 1924:

> *"While at Bridgend, Gronow, not satisfied with Saturday matches, played on Wednesdays also. It was in one of these latter games that he first came across Johnny Rogers, then a midget of fourteen, and was generally struck by his play. Shortly afterwards, when dressing for a match at Bridgend, he was told that one of their wing-three-quarters could not play. Happening to look out of the window he saw Johnny amongst the small*

crowd of enthusiasts who were waiting to watch the team go down to the field. Ben sent for Johnny and asked him if he would fill the vacant place. Johnny nearly collapsed with astonishment, but when he recovered jumped at the chance. The next difficulty was to find clothes and boots small enough. One wag threw Johnny a pair of boots belonging to the nineteen-stone man, Griffiths. Eventually suitable raiment was unearthed, and though the fourteen-year-old was all but lost to sight on the field, he played so well that he was afterwards selected as first reserve amongst the backs. He had to wait some weeks ere his chance came. Then he deputised for one of the halves and to such purpose that the man for whom he played understudy never got back, and Rogers commenced an uninterrupted partnership with Clem Lewis which continued, first with Bridgend and then with Cardiff, until he came to Huddersfield."

Rogers graduated from Bridgend to Cardiff in season 1911-12 and made his debut for the blue and blacks in a 6-0 home win over Gloucester on March 23rd. According to club records he made 35 first team appearances for Cardiff before going north. At Cardiff he played alongside such notable Internationals as Louis Dyke, Billy Spiller, Ewan Davies, W.J. Jenkins and his fellow townie, the celebrated Clem Lewis, winner of eleven Welsh caps and a great stand-off, who served the Cardiff club for 14 years. Johnny twice played against Billy Millar's South African touring side in 1912-13. The first occasion was somewhat traumatic as the Springboks, fired by four tries from winger Jan Stegmann, ran Glamorgan ragged with a 35-3 triumph at Swansea. The second game against Cardiff was a much closer affair as Johnny kicked a penalty to add to Spiller's try in a 6-7 victory for the Springboks, who scored a penalty and a drop-goal. Under modern scoring values the result would have been 7-6 to Cardiff! Johnny's prowess with the boot was to the fore in games against Cardiff & District Union and against Bristol when each yielded him eight conversions.

Johnny Rogers signed for Huddersfield on March 1st, 1913 and played his first game the same day. Although he was completely mystified by much of what went on in the game against Bramley at Fartown that day, the Huddersfield officials, spectators and players knew that at £100 the club had a rare bargain. Huddersfield's team of supermen beat Bramley 73-5 and Johnny had an easy introduction to his new code announcing his intent with three tries and a goal.

Rogers was twenty years old at the time of his capture by Huddersfield. Small (5' 4" and 10 $^1/_2$ stones), dapper and whippet-quick, Johnny was ideally suited to either half-back position under the Northern Union laws. Harold Wagstaff, most revered of all league players and an astute judge of ability, wrote of his little colleague in 1934:

"The best scrum-halves I have seen in RL football have been Chris McKivatt, captain of the 1911 Australians . . . . , Johnny Rogers, Jonty

Parkin and Fred Smith. McKivatt was a wonderful forager for the ball and so was Jonty Parkin. The two similar in type were glorious generals for they controlled the team from the scrum-half position. Johnny Rogers was the best attacking half of all – I have no wish to see a better – and Fred Smith, a scrum-half in a class of his own, was wonderfully strong and a tireless worker".

In 1936 Wagstaff wrote:

"Often I have marvelled at the way in which Johnny Rogers, the fastest of attacking scrum-halves the rugby game has known, worked when he was in our side. Rogers was always placed correctly at the scrum and there was the start for his brilliantly fast action, the like of which we may never see again. Rogers was wonderfully quick into his stride and his dash often took him through the defence and up to the full-back before the defence knew what had happened. His speed off the mark was phenomenal; but do not forget that he always gave himself a chance because he wasted no time in getting hold of that ball when his forwards heeled it".

Wagstaff's great international partner Billy Batten, later a team-mate of Johnny at Wakefield, used to say it was something akin to purgatory defending against the quicksilver Welshman. *"You know"*, he would say, *"in addition to having to watch the centres we have to keep an eye on that little ..... who's so fast that he's through you before you know where you are, unless you watch him all the time".*

Johnny Rogers was not the first Welsh half-back to grace the claret and gold livery of the Huddersfield club for a fellow Bridgend player had joined the Fartowners in 1905. This had been Will Hopkins who failed to make a real impression. At the time of Johnny's signing, however, the Huddersfield half-back positions were held by two brilliant Welshmen. Jim Davies had come north for £140 in 1905 from Swansea. He had originally been a centre but after two years had gone back to Wales. When Huddersfield played at Merthyr Tydfil on January 18th, 1908 Davies was persuaded to take the stand-off role and never looked back. As Stanley Chadwick wrote in *"Claret and Gold"* in 1946:

"In this position Davies revealed himself a masterful strategist and tactician, and his triangular exchanges with Harold Wagstaff became the talk of Northern Union football . . . . The famous triangular exchanges . . . . which became known as the 'standing pass', has had many imitators, but few have been successful in obtaining the full points of the two inventors. In this movement Davies, receiving the ball from the scrum-half, transferred it to Wagstaff. Before the Huddersfield captain could be tackled, Davies would receive the ball on the other side. In making the transfer Wagstaff turned his back on his opponent's goal. The two players had to meet the charge that the movement was 'scientific obstruction', but this was not the case".

Jim Davies

Davies earned the game's highest honours, appearing in two test matches against the 1911-12 Australians, winning three Welsh caps and gaining selection for the first Australasian tour in 1910. On December 22nd, 1909 Davies was joined at Fartown by Tommy Grey, a scrum-half of great repute who had joined Halifax from Swansea in 1906. At Halifax Grey had developed a telepathic half-back partnership with Jimmy Hilton and shared many triumphs with the Thrum Hall side. It took £50 to prise Grey away from Thrum Hall to Fartown, where the two Swansea men were to form such a brilliant partnership. Grey also won three Welsh caps and was a notable goal-kicker. In 1911-12 he set up a Fartown record by landing 96 goals and became the first Welshman to pass 200 points in Northern Union history when he claimed 219. That season was Huddersfield's first really great campaign and Davies and Grey were at the heart of Fartown's effort. Both played in winning teams in the Championship Final when Wigan were vanquished 13-5 at Halifax and in the Yorkshire Cup Final when Hull Kingston went down 22-12 at Wakefield. Only four games were lost in the league as the club topped the table. The Yorkshire League Championship fell to the Fartowners and only defeat at Oldham in the third round of the Challenge Cup prevented Huddersfield from sweeping the board clean. In league matches alone 996 points were amassed as wingers Abe Rosenfeld and Stanley Moorhouse swept in for 78 and 48 tries respectively.

It can be seen therefore that Johnny Rogers had to be something extraordinary to gain a place in such company. Joining the side in the later stages of 1912-13 he had to play second fiddle to the Davies-Grey combination as Huddersfield again took the Championship, the Yorkshire League Championship and the Challenge Cup. Only the Yorkshire Cup eluded this almost perfect rugby machine.

Season 1913-14 saw Johnny replace Grey as Davies' partner in crime and there were over 100 points to his credit by the end of the campaign. He opened the season by kicking nine goals in a 54-14 win at York on September 6th and a week later scored one of the finest tries ever seen on the Fartown ground in a 31-10 drubbing of Leeds. On November 29th at Halifax Johnny shared with fellow Welshmen Gronow, Davies and John Chilcott (ex-Ogmore Vale) in the Yorkshire Cup Final victory over Bradford Northern to win his first medal. George Todd, a reserve winger standing in for Moorhouse, scored a record four tries in a 19-3 win. For the third successive year the Yorkshire League was won and once again the club finished at the top of the league. Salford, however, took the Championship with a 5-3 verdict over the Fartowners in the Final at Headingley, where a few weeks earlier Wagstaff's men had again been taken by surprise when Hull removed them from the Challenge Cup competition with an 11-3 triumph before 30,000 fans.

This was the season that Abe Rosenfeld, the diminutive Australian winger with the lethal finishing power, set up the RL try-scoring record

Tommy Grey

which seems liable to last for ever. Little Abe ran in 80 touchdowns. His centre and fellow Aussie, Tommy Gleeson could only manage 45 tries!

For Johnny the season held his first Welsh cap and was climaxed by his selection for the Australasian Tour of 1914 along with his team-mates Wagstaff, Moorhouse , Clark, Chilcott and Fred Longstaff. A fractured shoulder sustained against Rochdale Hornets before Christmas almost certainly cost Gronow his place on the tour although Ben managed to get back into action in time for the Championship.

Both Rogers and Gronow went on the 1920 Tour which turned sour for Johnny when he fractured his left leg at Auckland on July 24th. Johnny had played in all three tests against Australia, figuring on the wing in the third test at Sydney when the tourists won 23-13. He kicked three goals in that match. Ben Gronow played in two of the Australian tests and in all three in New Zealand and set up new scoring records for a tour by kicking 65 goals and claiming 136 points in 16 appearances. Ben went on a second tour in 1924 but injuries restricted him to eight appearances during which he kicked five goals and scored one try and he did not make the test side.

Coincidentally both these sons of Bridgend made seven test appearances but were only in the same side twice – the first and second tests in Australia in 1920 both of which were lost. Ben Gronow played eight games for Wales between 1910 and 1923 and captained his country on a couple of occasions. He also made two appearances for Other Nationalities against England. Johnny Rogers gained three Welsh caps and one for Other Nationalities and had to compete with some marvellous Welsh players for half-back honours. Among his contemporaries were Bobby Lloyd and Stuart Prosser of Halifax (both ex-Pontypool), Wigan's great triumvirate of Johnny Thomas (ex-Maesteg & Cardiff), Sid Jerram and George Owens (both ex-Swansea), Hull's Eddie Caswell (ex-Cardiff) and, of course, Jim Davies and Tommy Grey.

Returning to the subject of domestic football, Huddersfield dazzled more brightly than ever in 1914-15, reaching unparalleled heights of brilliance. The machine driven by the divine Wagstaff was virtually unstoppable and the quality of their play was breathtaking. In 1907-08 Hunslet, under the "King of Drop-goals", Albert Goldthorpe, had become the first club to win all four major trophies in a single season. Hunslet met Huddersfield at Fartown in the semi-final of the Yorkshire Cup on November 14th, 1914. Such encounters are usually characteristically dour, defence-dominated affairs but this Huddersfield team was a team apart from any other and ran riot to win by 64-3, the highest score ever recorded at the semi-final stage of any first-class competition in English RL. Hull probably felt they had been let off comparatively lightly in the final at Headingley on November 28th when the Fartowners won 31-0. Ben Gronow had not yet taken over the goal-kicking role but there was a try for Rogers. Twenty-four games were played in the Yorkshire

League, none of which were lost although four were drawn and so the title went to Fartown for the fourth year running.

Only two league games were lost out of 34 and Huddersfield finished in their accustomed place at the head of the table. The Championship semi-final with Rochdale ended in a 33-2 thrashing for the Hornets but Leeds who were to meet Wagstaff and Co in the final at Wakefield believed they had the answer to the Fartown juggernaut. Their plan, simple in the extreme, consisted of heavy spotting of the magical Huddersfield backs to prevent Huddersfield from indulging in their customary free-flowing movements. The Loiners followed their instructions with the result that within a very short space of time three tries had been score by the Fartown pack, who could also play rugby, Gronow, Clark and Longstaff crossing. Ben Gronow had a field day with seven goals and two tries giving him 20 points as Leeds were deluged 35-2. Rogers again scored a try.

On May 1st, 1915 at Oldham in the Challenge Cup Final Huddersfield swept aside a puny St. Helens, recording the biggest winning margin in Cup Final history – 37-3.

Ben Gronow kicked five goals and scored a try and Johnny Rogers kept up his record with his third try in as many finals in that record-shattering season.

Thus all four cups were won with a style and *panache* missing from the Hunslet and Swinton (1927-28) teams which also accomplished this difficult feat.

When competitive rugby resumed after the horrors of the Great War Huddersfield carried on where they had left off winning everything except the Championship which was conceded to Hull by a 3-2 score-line in 1920. Ben and Johnny, along with Gwyn Thomas, Waggie and Clark missed the match as they were *en route* for the Antipodes. Although there were still finals to be contested by the Fartowners in the early 1920s the Team of All the Talents steadily began to break up and in 1924-25 Ben Gronow left the scene of his triumphs to take up a coaching position in Australia where he stayed for a couple of years before returning to Fartown. In 1928-29 he served three clubs – Huddersfield, Batley and Featherstone Rovers. His last game was for the Rovers v Leeds on 16th November, 1929.

Johnny Rogers also played his last game for Huddersfield in 1924-25 before moving on to Wakefield Trinity in January 1925 for a fee of £300. What a bargain the tiny terror had been for Huddersfield who recouped three times the amount they paid for his services. At Wakefield he resumed his sublime partnership with Jonty Parkin, arguably English Rugby League's greatest half-back and his old Test associate.

However, it is for their great deeds with that heaven-sent Huddersfield team of all teams that Gronow and Rogers will be best remembered. As the author of Ben Gronow's benefit brochure wrote in 1924:

Five great Fartowners for the 1920 Tour.
Ben Gronow, Harold Wagstaff, Johnny Rogers, Gwyn Thomas, Douglas Clark

"There was something about the Huddersfield team of that period that carried people out of themselves. It was not merely the successes which impressed; it was the manner in which they were gained. There was an absolute understanding between all parts of a perfectly-working machine which resulted in the most audacious and unexpected movements being carried out with a precision that left the opposing defence aghast. Fast and clever three-quarters were served by halves whose brains were ever working at high pressure behind forwards who, as occasion demanded, could play the traditional scrummaging game or convert themselves into temporary three-quarters and handle the ball with a precision that would put to shame many of our present-day backs. Truly a great side and, so far as humanly possible, without a weak spot – a team of giants who loved the game, gloried in a stern struggle, and cared not who put on the finishing touches to a movement so long as each did his share of what fell to his lot to do".

BEN GRONOW'S PLAYING RECORD FOR HUDDERSFIELD

	GAMES	TRIES	GOALS	POINTS
1910-11	31	6	8	34
1911-12	41	12	11	58
1912-13	37	10	—	30
1913-14	32	7	1	23
1914-15	43	4	140	292
1918-19	4	1	12	27
1919-20	42	12	147	330
1920-21	33	6	53	124
1921-22	38	9	79	185
1922-23	38	7	100	221
1923-24	33	6	70	158
1924-25	20	—	46	92
1927-28	1	—	1	2
1928-29	2	—	5	10
TOTALS	395	80	673	1,586

All first-class matches:

	474	86	826	1,910

JOHNNY ROGERS' PLAYING RECORD FOR HUDDERSFIELD

	GAMES	TRIES	GOALS	POINTS
1912-13	6	5	1	17
1913-14	41	20	27	114
1914-15	39	26	4	86
1918-19	4	3	—	9
1919-20	39	21	—	63
1920-21	17	2	—	6
1921-22	37	11	5	43
1922-23	38	9	5	37
1923-24	38	9	—	27
1924-25	3	—	—	—
TOTALS	262	106	42	402

All first-class matches:

	342	119	60	477

Chapter 2

Joe Thompson
(Cross Keys RU, Leeds RL)

Joseph Francis Thompson won his solitary Welsh Rugby Union cap at Twickenham on January 20th, 1923 having passed his twentieth birthday less than a month previously. Three months later he was a member of Leeds Rugby League Challenge Cup winning side and by October, 1923 he had become a dual Welsh International having won his first League cap against England.

A less likely candidate for such honours in such a rapid succession is difficult to envisage. To begin with Thompson was born in England – at Hambrook, Gloucestershire – and both his parents were English. Not that being born in England has ever proved a major stumbling block to selection for the Welsh national side at Union when players from Frank Hancock (instigator of the four three-quarter system in 1884) to John Taylor (scourge of the Scots in 1971) have had the misfortune to be born on the wrong side of the border. The Thompson family migrated to Wales, however, when Joe was in his early infancy and he grew up in Cross Keys.

As if his English birth were not hindrance enough to prospects of a Welsh cap Thompson had never played a game of rugby until his late teens. His conversion to the handling game was a fortuitous accident for he became disillusioned at being unable to gain a first team place in his local soccer club and threw in his lot with Abercarn Rugby Club. It was not long before he was playing for Cross Keys, however, and proving that he was born to be a rugby forward. Although now no longer a great power among the top Welsh clubs, the Cross Keys of the inter-war period certainly was a top-ranking club. In Thompson's only full season at Pandy Park (1921-22) Cross Keys were winners of the unofficial Welsh Championship and boasted Internationals such as full-back Ossie Male, scrum-half Freddie Reeves and forwards Steve Winmill and the celebrated Steve Morris, who with 19 caps was the most-capped Welshman of the 1920s.

For Thompson to have won an International cap with such a limited amount of experience marked him an exceptional talent and that talent was duly noted by the scouts of the Leeds club. Within three weeks of the International at Twickenham, which Wales lost by 3-7 to a stupendous drop-goal from Leicester winger Alastair Smallwood, Thompson had signed for Leeds and embarked upon an honour-laden and record-breaking Rugby League career. His signing-on fee was £300 and he did not hesitate to take the offer. He had been a miner from the age of thirteen

Joe Thompson

and on his own admission could not wait to escape from the pit. The Welsh Rugby Union made him wait for his cap, however, which he received fifty-two years after he won it.

As a Union forward Thompson had been something of a short-line-out specialist but could not really define his position as it was still a case of "first man up, first man down" in the 1920s. As a League player, however, he invariably figured in the second-row. Thompson was a terrific tackler, a tireless forager, a straight runner and could give a good pass. His favourite pursuit, however, was dribbling for which there was still considerable scope in League but which is nowadays to all intents and purposes a lost art. Joe loved to dribble for the simple reason that with the ball at his feet he could not be tackled.

Apart from possessing all the qualities needed by a top-class forward Joe Thompson was a master goal-kicker who won many a game for the Headingley side and whose name is writ large in the Leeds scoring records. By the time he retired in 1933 he had kicked 862 goals and scored 1,883 points for the Loiners, records which have only been surpassed by one Leeds player – Lewis Jones. In 1925-26 Joe set a seasonal record of 87 goals for the club and broke his own record a further three times in 1927-28 (102 goals), in 1929-30 (110) and in 1930-31 (112). The latter record stood until 1949-50 when New Zealander Bert Cook landed 115 goals. In all first-class League matches Thompson claimed 921 goals and exceeded 2,000 points. Although even Thompson would be the first to admit that no finer goal-kicker than Jim Sullivan ever laced on boots he had the unique distinction of heading "Peerless Jim" in the goal-kicking lists in two seasons (1927-28 and 1929-30). From 1921-22 until the outbreak of the Second World War Sullivan finished as top goal-kicker in every season but those two. Joe preferred to kick with a pointed ball whereas Sullivan liked the rounder type of leather in a period when ball shape and size were somewhat haphazard. Joe always pointed the ball toward the goal and the farther the kick the flatter he placed it. His run was relatively short. His largest haul in a single game was eleven goals in a 61-3 victory over Bradford Northern on November 11th, 1925, a game in which ex-Penarth centre Mel Rosser grabbed five tries and Jim Bacon (ex-Cross Keys) four tries. A month earlier Joe had scored 10 goals and two tries in a game against Bramley. He also hit the ten goal mark during the 1932 Tour of Australasia in a game against Wide-Bay.

Thompson played his first game for Leeds against Huddersfield at Headingley on 10th February, 1923, a game which was won narrowly (6-3) and he hardly missed a game in the next ten years. A powerful constitution (5' 10" and around 15 stones in his prime) no doubt helped him withstand the hurly-burly of the forward exchanges but he also had the good fortune not to suffer from any major injuries throughout his career. In only the 16th game of his professional career Joe Thompson became proud possessor of a Challenge Cup winners' medal as Leeds

Mel Rosser – ex Penarth. 2 Welsh RU caps.
Signed for Leeds in 1924.Subsequently played for York.
Australasian Tour 1928.

Evan Williams – ex Aberavon, 2 Welsh RU caps.
Signed by Leeds in 1925 and made over 400 appearances for the club.

defeated Hull 28-3 in the final at Wakefield with his own contribution being five goals. The game was so one-sided that it was described as Leeds' easiest round in the competition. Joe collected a second winners' medal in the 1932 final, which was the last not to be played at Wembley (excluding war-time). The venue was Central Park, Wigan and Leeds' opponents were Swinton. By now Thompson was captain of his team which contained a galaxy of stars from both hemispheres including three Australian three-quarters in Eric Harris, Jeff Moores and Frank O'Rourke, ex-England Rugby Union full-back Jim Brough and Evan Williams (ex-Aberavon and Wales RU). Unlike Thompson's previous Cup Final there was nothing one-sided about this one. Leeds led 8-2 at half-time thanks to four penalty goals from Joe kicked between the eighth and twentieth minutes and with the help of a high wind. Joe's counterpart in the Swinton pack Martyn Hodgson, one of Rugby League's greatest forwards also kicked four penalties before the game ended but Joe's had been the more crucial as he had "got mine in first". The real match decider, however, has been the only try of the game which had fallen to Eric Harris, "The Toowoomba Ghost", and the finest winger Thompson ever saw. Harris had earned his nick-name from his ability to change pace imperceptibly and so ghost past would-be tacklers and it this ability which carried him past winger Kenny and full-back Scott in a run over half the length of the pitch to clinch the match.

Having joined a club as successful as Leeds it was perhaps inevitable that Thompson should capture most of the game's honours for apart from his two Challenge Cup medals he also took part in two Yorkshire Cup Finals both of which yielded him winners' medals. In 1928 he kicked a goal to add to Frank O'Rourke's try scored after the opposing full-back made a mullock of a Leeds kick through as Leeds beat Featherstone Rovers 5-0 in atrocious conditions at Wakefield. Two years later the County Cup fell again to the Loiners who defeated Huddersfield 10-2 at Halifax. Thompson landed a couple of goals and the game ended with Leeds Scottish forward Jimmie Douglas and Huddersfield captain Bowkett being sent off. Leeds won the Yorkshire League Championship in 1927-28 and 1930-31 and were also runners-up four times during Thompson's time at Headingley. The one medal he could not get his hands on was a Rugby League Championship Winners although Leeds appeared in three consecutive Championship Finals in 1929, 1930 and 1931. Huddersfield beat them in the first two finals by 2-0 and 10-0 (after a replay) and Swinton triumphed 14-7 in 1931, an occasion on which Martin Hodgson outkicked Thompson by four goals to two although Joe had the mortification of hitting the post twice within five minutes. The Leeds scrum-half J. Fawcett made his debut in this match, a unique occurrence. It was to be 1961 before a Leeds side lifted the Championship.

Joe's representative career in League began almost immediately and spanned 25 tests and internationals. He also played seven times for the

Joe Thompson

BIG JOE THOMPSON, of England, pulls 'em apart to see how they are made! Fine forward is Joe!

HARRY CAMPBELL

Welsh Team versus England at Pontypridd, April 12th, 1926

Back row: Mr. Edmund Osborne (Warrington), and Mr. J.F. Whittaker (Batley)

Standing: Harry Rees (reserve - Batley), Dai Edwards (reserve - Rochdale), F.L. Roffey (St. Helens), Edgar Morgan (Hull),

Rev. Frank H. Chambers (Dewsbury - Referee), Wilf Hodder (Wigan), Joe Thompson (Leeds), Mr. Leake and Mr. Wilf M Gabbatt (Barrow).

Sitting: Bryn Philips (Huddersfield), Joe Jones (Leeds), Ike Fowler (Batley), Jim Sullivan (Wigan - Captain),

Mel. Rosser (Leeds), Dai Rees (Halifax) and Jim Bacon (Leeds)

In front: Frank Evans (Swinton) and W. "Billo" Rees (Swinton).

old Glamorgan & Monmouthshire side in the County Championship. He kicked only eight goals in all these games as his services in the kicking department were superfluous as Jim Sullivan was a fixture in all those teams. Joe had the unfortunate experience of never playing for a winning Welsh team at either code, his eight RL games for Wales all ending in defeats, seven of which were again England. Although he never appeared at Wembley in a Cup Final Joe did play there on one occasion. This was on January 18th, 1930 when he captained Wales for the first and only time against Australia but despite putting out a pack of outstanding forwards such as Billy Williams (Salford), Les White (Hunslet), Frank Stephens (Wigan), Candy Evans (Leeds) and Jesse Meredith (Warrington) the Welsh went down 26-10 to Tom Gorman's Kangaroos. Although Joe captained Leeds on numerous occasions he positively disliked captaining the international side as he felt it restricted his own game. Whilst Joe never ended up on a winning side for Wales he did figure in two victories over England by Other Nationalities sides scoring a try in a 23-17 triumph at Headingley in 1924 and being content to watch others do the scoring in a 35-19 win at Halifax in 1930.

In the higher sphere of test football Joe Thompson stood out as one of his era's best and most durable forwards. He played in twelve tests, only four of which were lost. Strangely enough only one of his tests took place in England and that was a disaster for Britain who went down 31-8 to Australia in the first test of 1929 at Hull. Of his other tests five were played in Australia and six in New Zealand. Joe had the remarkable distinction of participating in three tours of Australasia in 1924, 1928 and 1932. At the time of his third trip he was the only forward to have accomplished this feat and only one other forward has emulated him since. This was Workington Town's Brian Edgar who toured in 1958, 1962 and 1966. On each of Thompson's tours the British won the Ashes. His records on the three tours were:

	GAMES	TRIES	GOALS
1924	18	6	17
1928	14	4	14
1932	15	—	12

Joe never had any qualms about going on any of the tours but was somewhat lucky to make the 1928 tour as he was not among the original selections. He was however invited to take the place of his Leeds teammate, the ungainly but stunningly effective loose-forward Frank Gallagher, who withdrew from the party. Ironically it would have been Gallagher's third tour. Joe had played in the second test at Sydney in 1924 when the Ashes were clinched with a 5-3 victory thanks to captain Jonty Parkin's try. Joe felt he was extremely fortunate to get a test place as there were any number of superb forwards in the party. He also played in two of the tests in New Zealand but both were lost. On the 1928 tour Thompson played in the second Australian test (won 8-0 at Sydney) and the third New Zealand test (won 6-5 at Christchurch). It was the final tour, however, which was most memorable for Thompson and of the three parties this was probably the most talented, especially among the backs. Captain of the side was the redoubtable Jim Sullivan and he had at his disposal a three-quarter line which it is difficult to imagine has ever been surpassed for speed and skill. The wings were St. Helens' Alf Ellaby (445 tries in his career) and Thompson's fellow Loiner Stanley Smith. Their centre partners were Huddersfield's spring-heeled Stanley Brogden and Castleford's rumbustuous Arthur 'Bluss' Atkinson. Salford's Gus Risman was making his first tour and had to content himself with the stand-off position in two of the tests. The forwards read like a "Who's Who" of pack play and Thompson had to compete for a place with the likes of Martin Hodgson, Bill Horton, A.E. Fildes, Jack Feetham, Nat Silcock and fellow Welsh Internationals Norman Fender and Billy Williams. The only forwards to play in all six tests were Thompson and his old adversary Martin Hodgson. The first test against Australia produced a world record crowd for a League match when 70, 204 fans packed themselves into the Sydney Cricket Ground to witness an 8-6 victory for the tourists, all the scoring coming in the first half. The second test was probably the toughest game of rugby Joe ever played and was subsequently dubbed the "Battle of Brisbane". The game was a brutally fought blood-bath which began sensationally with Australian scrum-half Hec Gee (later to play for Wigan) scoring a converted try before the British had even touched the ball. There was no way Australia were going to surrender their lead and the series in this game. From the very first scrum sparks began to fly and Joe Thompson was carried senseless from the field to be followed by a succession of bloodied, bruised and battered colleagues and opponents. Miraculously Mr. J. Simpson, the referee, never actually sent anyone off even though the mayhem went unabated. In terms of injuries the Aussies were the more cruelly afflicted. Dan Dempsey, one of Australia's toughest second-rowers of any era but playing hooker in this little *téte-a-téte*, fractured his wrist, stand-off Eric Weissel severely damaged an ankle but contrived to run or hobble 75 yards late in the game to set up the winning try for Gee, who himself had previously been knocked cold and had to have his lip stitched. Nineteen year-old centre, Ernie Norman, playing in his first test series was laid out three times and suffered severe concussion whilst loose-forward Frank O'Connor (normally a half-back) suffered a grue-somely cut eye and full-back Frank McMillan also was knocked sense-less. The British got off comparatively lightly with Martin Hodgson sustaining a wickedly gashed eye, ex-Pontypridd RL hooker Les White needing stitches to his scalp and Thompson's Leeds team-mate and scrum-half "Juicey" Adams joining the ranks of the senseless. The net

Dai (D.R.) Jenkins – ex Swansea, 2 Welsh RU caps.
Signed by Leeds in 1928-29

result was a 15-6 victory for the Aussies but the British won the war.

The brutality of the "Battle of Brisbane" is hard to account for even allowing for the traditional ferocity of Anglo-Aussie clashes. The first test had been played in good spirit and the third was also to be fairly contested. Joe Thompson certainly could never account for the eruption of bad-temper maintaining that the game just flared up and never cooled down. His assertion was that there were no really dirty players around in his day as the forwards, at least, were always too busy to fight as they were never done scrummaging as anything up to eighty scrums a game was the order of the day.

The third test of 1932 was Thompson's swan-song as far as the Aussies were concerned but the song was a triumphant one as Britain retained the Ashes with an 18-13 triumph after trailing 9-3 at the interval. Half of the British pack were Welsh (Williams, White and Thompson) and two of the backs (Risman and Sullivan) but it was a Yorkshireman, the flying wing Stanley Smith who put the skids under Australia with a hat-trick of tries. Joe played in all three of the tests that followed in New Zealand in which the Kiwis were "whitewashed" 24-9, 25-14, 20-18. Only two of the 26 tour games were lost including that notorious "Battle of Brisbane".

It was on the tour of 1932 that Joe was sent off for the only time in a game at Newcastle, New South Wales which the tourists won 22-15. To this day no-one, least of all Joe, knows why he received his marching orders as he had just received a kick in the midriff.

Joe played his last game at Featherstone Rovers on April 29th, 1933, a game that Leeds won 16-15. Leeds paid him the signal honour of making him an Honorary Life Member of the club. Perhaps Alfred Drewry, the eminent Rugby League correspondent of *"The Yorkshire Post"*, most fittingly eulogised Thompson when he wrote:

> *"Never was there a man less likely to have his head turned by fame or flattery. His approach to life was like his approach to football – simple, direct, thoughtful and sincere. There was something reassuringly solid about that massive figure, that firmly moulded beak of a nose and that determined, jutting jaw, its severity relieved by the bald patch which gave him an air almost scholarly. Joe Thompson was dependability itself. From the day at Twickenham when their scouts saw a young forward from Cwmcarn walk to the touchline, spit out a few broken teeth, and then go back into the game as though it was nothing at all out of the ordinary, Leeds knew that they were on a good thing".* ("Rugby League Review", July 12th 1951).

JOE THOMPSON'S PLAYING RECORD FOR LEEDS

	GAMES	TRIES	GOALS	POINTS
1922-23	16	2	24	54
1923-24	30	10	63	156
1924-25	35	4	51	114
1925-26	37	8	87	198
1926-27	39	6	63	144
1927-28	43	7	102	225
1928-29	32	1	75	153
1929-30	40	7	110	241
1930-31	45	3	112	233
1931-32	36	4	99	210
1932-33	37	1	76	155
TOTALS	390	53	862	1,883

All first-class matches:

	462	67	921	2,043

Chapter 3

Gus Risman
(Cardiff Scottish RU, Salford RL, Workington Town RL, Batley RL)

Augustus John was Wales' greatest portrait painter and it is therefore fitting that one of the most creative of Welsh rugby men should also have borne that name. Augustus John Risman's contribution to and achievements in the game of Rugby League were truly monumental. In the history of the game only four men kicked more goals than Risman; only two – Sullivan and Fox – scored more points; only Sullivan played more first-class games. Even the perenniel Sullivan did not last as long as Gus in this toughest of sports for "Big Jim's" career spanned 24 $\frac{1}{2}$ years whereas from first to last Risman's covered 25 years and four months – the longest career known in first-class Rugby League. This Methusela of the game played his last game for Batley in 1954 at the age of 43 years and 279 days. Sullivan, a stripling in comparison, had bowed out at 42 years 83 days.

Three Australian tours, the last as captain, 36 test and International caps, three Wembley Challenge Cup Finals, five Ashes-winning series, six winning Championship Finals, four victorious Lancashire Cup Finals, five Lancashire League Championship winners' medals, a Yorkshire Cup winners' laurels, 873 matches, 232 tries, 1,678 goals, 4,052 points, captaincy of the British Army XV and the Welsh Services XV during the Second World War – the bare bones of the Risman saga are impressive enough. They do not, however, paint the complete picture of this brilliantly gifted exponent of the thirteen-a-side code. They give no indication of what a versatile performer he was at full-back, centre or stand-off for he was expert in all those positions and played tests in all three. Figures cannot convey the athleticism, thoughtfulness and cunning that accompanied him on the field. His demeanour on the field, his umblemished discipline over a quarter of a century and his impeccable leadership marked him out as a model sportsman and earned him the respect of his opponents and the worship of the fans.

A few months before his retirement a critic was moved to write:

> "It is for us to make the most of this Risman while we can . . . He was to be seen at Knowsley Road a few weeks ago tripping easily and skilfully through a game in the masterly fashion he has been doing for nearly a generation. The same familiar movement of the classical athlete; the efficiency of a well-oiled machine; the energy of a man half his age; the conservation of energy which is the mark of all great artistes; the skill which has made him a legend in Rugby League history. A big, strong man, Risman

Gus Risman leads out Workington Town.

used his physical attributes when he found strength and weight necessary but more generally he preferred to charm us with the sly dummy, the scintillating side-step, the acceleration through the half-opening seen out of the corner of an eye as sharp as a hawk's, or with the beautifully timed and brilliantly judged drop-goal that took the heart out of the most solid of defences. With a ball in his hands Risman was possibly the most capable all-round footballer the Rugby League has seen, and his defence was like a stone wall, his tackling devastating in its power and quality".

Like many another player who went north to seek fame and fortune Gus Risman hailed from the Tiger Bay area of Cardiff, where he was born on March 23rd, 1911. As a boy attending South Church Street School he was rugby-mad but the Risman family left Cardiff for Barry when he was eleven and he had to attend the soccer-playing Gladstone Road School. He developed into such a good soccer player that he had a Welsh Schools' trial at the age of thirteen. He was saved for the handling code, however, on winning a scholarship to the Barry County School where rugby was the game.

Gus' career in Union was extremely short – a few games for Dinas Powis and Cardiff Scottish. Economic pressures determined that the young Risman should go north following an approach by Frank Young, the ex-Cardiff full-back and Northern Union tourist of 1910. Young had originally approached Gus with a view to recommending him to Leeds but the Headingley club were not short of quality backs at that time and so it was arranged for Gus to trial at Salford, who were just beginning to emerge from a long period in the doldrums thanks to the dynamism and expertise of their manager, Lance Todd.

Gus signed for Salford on January 31st, 1929, a couple of months before his 18th birthday. In his autobiography Risman relates that his signing fee was £52 to be paid at £1 per week over the following year. At the time Gus' father was very ill and on hearing of this Lance Todd threw in another £25 in cash. So for £77 plus match fees of £3 for an win and £1/15/- for a defeat Salford bought one of the greatest talents to grace the game of professional rugby. It was not a moment too soon for Cardiff RU was keen to acquire his services and Tottenham Hotspur had been hot on his trail.

Gus' introduction to League came via the Salford "A" team and he had an inauspicious start to his career breaking an ankle in one of his first matches. At the start of the 1929-30 season, however, he was thrown in with the big boys, making his debut on the right wing on August 31st in a home match against Barrow. Gus scored a try from an interception and, metaphorically, never looked back. His next game was at full-back and so well did he take his opportunity that in his first season he only missed one game. Within three months of his debut he found himself playing in the Final of the Lancashire Cup, the first of 18 finals in his career. On this

occasion he was to suffer disappointment as Warrington defeated Salford 15-2.

For the first couple of seasons that Gus spent at the Willows he was
used as a full-back but with Jim Sullivan established in the Glamorgan &
Monmouthshire, Welsh and test teams his prospects of representative
honours were slight. The selectors, however, clearly saw his talents and
he was chosen at centre for Glamorgan and Monmouthshire on his own
ground at Salford for the game with Yorkshire on November 22nd, 1930.
His county debut yielded him a try as the Welshmen beat the Tykes 14-
10. A few months later he made another try-scoring debut as a centre on
March 31st, 1931, a week after his 20th birthday. The venue was Fartown,
Huddersfield and Risman was wearing the red shirt of Wales for the first
time against England. His co-centre that day was the ex-Penarth and
Wales RU star Mel Rosser (York). Risman was to play 18 international
matches for Wales (plus one for England when he scored two tries
against France in that country's first international in 1934). Strangely
enough all his Welsh caps were gained as a centre, often in partnership
to his club winger Alan Edwards who benefitted so much from Risman's
unselfish service. Risman's long raking gait made him appear deceptively slow but once away he was not often caught, and he had a curious
little jink, part side-step and part swerve, which created the gaps from
which he unleashed the hare-quick Edwards. The Edwards-Risman
combination for Salford, Wales and Great Britain would bear comparison with any other wing-centre partnership of any era. The pair played
together for Wales for ten years including the International Championship winning seasons of 1935-6, 1936-7 and 1937-8 when a glorious Welsh
team went undefeated. Risman captained Wales on his last five appearances, Sullivan at last having relinquished his monopoly on the steward-
ship. His final game was fittingly triumphant as Wales vanquished
England 11-3 at Swansea in November 1945 in the first post-war international match.

Season 1931-32 was especially memorable for Gus. He was still
playing much of his football at full-back and figured in that position in
a dramatic Lancashire Cup Final against arch rivals and near neighbours
Swinton at Broughton. Gus was able to claim his first winners' medal as
centre Fergie Southward kicked a last-gasp penalty to win the match 10-
8. At this stage in his career Risman was only being employed as an
occasional goal-kicker landing a mere 17 in three full seasons. 1932 was
to see the sixth British tour of Australasia and three tour trials were
therefore arranged. No-one doubted that Sullivan would be full-back
and most people believed that Jim Brough would be his deputy and it
certainly looked as if the selectors were thinking that way when Brough
was made captain of one of the teams for the first trial at Warrington.
Risman was in the same team at centre but for the second trial at Fartown
he was selected to play full-back opposite Brough and for the final trial

Gloucester 1942. War throws League and Union together.
The Welsh team which met England in a Services International.

Back row: A. Edwards (R.L., R.A.F.); V.J. Law (Newport, Army); R.E. Price (Weston, R.A.F.); R. Flowers (Pontypool); H. Payne (Swansea, Royal Navy);
T. Foster (R.L. and Army).
Sitting: T. Sullivan (Swansea, Army); C.H. Davies (Swansea, Army); L. Manfield (Cardiff, Army); A.J. Risman (R.L., Army) capt.; S. Williams (R.L., Army);
W.E.N. Davies (Cardiff, Army); G. Williams (R.L., Army).
Front row: W.T.H. Davies (R.L., R.A.F.); H. Tanner (Swansea, Army).

at Leeds he opposed the mighty Sullivan himself. He must have impressed for he was selected as reserve full-back to Sullivan and so won a place on the first of his trio of tours.

Risman did not expect to oust Sullivan from the test teams and the centre spots were the property of the brilliantly but diversely gifted Arthur Atkinson and Stan Brogden. The series stood level at one all when he finally received his test call-up and to everyone's surprise he was drafted in at stand-off for the Sydney decider. The match is described elsewhere but Risman's part must be mentioned. Britain found themselves 11-3 down soon after half-time at which point Risman and Brogden switched positions. Brogden, more used to playing at half-back than Gus and one of the fastest men in the game, began to create havoc in the Aussie defence and put Britain back in the match with a stunning try. Risman then served Stanley Smith whose try put the British in the lead for the first time. Australia came back to level the scores at 13-13 but with only minutes remaining Risman again unleashed the spring-heeled Smith who completed a hat-trick. Sullivan's touch-line conversion sealed an 18-13 victory and the Ashes were secured. Gus had proved his mettle and retained his spot for the three victorious tests in New Zealand in which he alternated with Brogden at centre and stand-off.

From his debut in test match football until his final test in 1946 Gus was never dropped and missed only one match through injury. In all he played in 17 tests – nine as captain – and experienced defeat in only one. Like Sullivan, he figured in five Ashes-winning series.

Gus played through the 1933 series against Australia at centre. Britain won three tight games 4-0, 7-5 and 19-16. In each test he had a different centre partner – Stan Brogden, Billy Dingsdale and Arthur Atkinson. By the time the 1936 tour party was to be selected there was little doubt that Gus would be in it. He was duly selected at centre and with him went four other Salford backs, three of whom – Alan Edwards, Billy Watkins and Emlyn Jenkins – were fellow Welshmen. The odd man out was an Englishman, barn-storming Barney Hudson, Risman's winger in two of the 1933 tests. The tour did not start too well for Risman suffered an ankle injury and missed the first test when the great Australian centre Dave Brown led the rampant Kangaroos to a 24-8 victory. He recovered in time to take his place in the second test at Brisbane when all four Salford Welsh played. The conditions were wet and treacherous and suited the Lions better than the Kangaroos. Edwards put Britain 3-0 up with a try in the corner and then Risman scored his first test points with a penalty goal before making a costly error in losing a ball which was picked up by the Aussie wing Archie Crippin who streaked 70 yards to level the scores. The crucial points came in the second half and were an all-Welsh affair. Emlyn Jenkins, the outstanding player of the series, had been making good use of an overwhelming supply of possession with some fine tactical kicking and it was from one of his kicks that Edwards scored his second try at the flag. Risman's magnificent conversion from the soggy touch-line was the killing blow and a 12-7 win levelled the series.

The third test at Sydney saw the tourists' captain Jim Brough out of the side and Gus was accorded the honour of leading the British team for the first time. This time all five Salford backs took the field. Australia drew first blood after 20 minutes when Brown landed a penalty goal but six other penalties went begging in the first half, which became spiteful at times, finally resulting in the dismissals of Madsen, the Kangaroo hooker and Arkwright, the Lions' second-row. Eventually the British began to dominate and Hudson's try from a cross-kick by Brogden enabled the Lions to lead 5-2 at the interval. Risman won the critics' acclaim for his inspirational leadership and some dreadnought defence, particularly for a tremendous tackle on winger Alan Ridley in the second half when he looked all over a scorer until Gus nailed him five yards out. Jenkins had the final word, clearing the way for Brogden to score and another 12-7 victory was the outcome. Gus received the Ashes trophy on his first appearance as British captain. He added to his laurels in New Zealand by leading the side to wins in both tests which were played in Auckland. The first was won 10-8 and the second 23-11 with four goals from Gus.

In 1937 Wally Prigg's Kangaroos came to England but lost the series 2-1. For the first and only time Risman experienced a test defeat when after sewing up the series with wins of 5-4 at Leeds and 13-3 as Swinton, Prigg's men surprised the British by taking the third test 13-3 at Huddersfield. There were to be another nine years and a world war before Anglo-Australian tests were resumed. By that time Gus Risman had passed his 35th birthday, a time when most players had called it a day and were happy to live on their memories. Gus was as fit and keen as ever, however, and when the 1946 tour party was announced he was named captain. There were no fewer than eleven Welshmen in the squad which became known as the "Indomitables" after the ship which carried the tourists to the Antipodes. "The Indomitable" was in fact an aircraft carrier which was taking Australian and New Zealand service-men home from the war.

By the time the first test was to be played both British full-backs were out of action (Martin Ryan and Joe Jones) and Risman was called upon to fill the position for the first time in a test. A stern struggle before almost 65,000 spectators ended in an 8-8 draw and Gus left his kicking boots in the dressing-room landing only one goal from nine attempts. For the second test at Brisbane Exhibition Ground there was great excitement and the gates had to be closed more than three hours before the kick-off with more than 40,000 fans inside the ground. Such was the crush outside the stadium the Australian team was unable to get into the ground, having to circle the stadium for 40 minutes before gaining admission

Gus Risman, followed by his Salford team-mates Alan Edwards, Barney Hudson, Emlyn Jenkins and Billy Watkins, leads out the Lions at Sydney, 1936.

through a rear gate! Ernest Ward, tour captain in 1950, took over at full-back allowing Risman to revert to centre to partner Arthur Bassett with Ted Ward as his co-centre. Winger Albert Johnson was the only non-Welsh three-quarter and half the pack in Frank Whitcombe, Doug Phillips and Ike Owens came from the valleys. Five tries were scored in the match and all went to wingers – three to Risman's partner Bassett, one to Johnson and one to Australia's Lionel Cooper as Britain ran out 14-5 winners. The third test at Sydney was anybody's as Britain led 10-7 with 16 minutes remaining. Australian full-back Dave Parkinson had been playing on a broken leg for most of the match and their hopes were shattered when second-rower Arthur Clues was ordered off with the Aussies only three points down. Late tries by Owens and Bassett gave Britain the Ashes and a 20-7 victory. It was a fitting end to Risman's great test career which had spanned 14 years, only Billy Batten having had a longer test career for Great Britain.

In domestic football Risman became king-pin of the enormously successful and entertaining Salford side of the thirties, so skilfully assembled and managed by Lance Todd. There was talent all through the side even if most of the glory was grabbed by the galaxy of stars that formed the back division. Welshmen were everywhere for apart from Risman the backs included at various times Jenkins, Watkins, Edwards and Albert Gear. In the forwards were ex-Union Internationals in Billy Williams, Bert Day, Harold (H.W.) Thomas and, latterly, Emrys Evans. Another great Welsh forward with the club was Aubrey Casewell, a native of Welshpool, who along with Williams, Day, Thomas, Evans and D.M. Davies all played for Wales at League. Billy Williams was one of the finest props to come out of Wales winning a place on the Australasian tours of 1928 and 1932. He was predecessor to Risman as captain and led Salford to many trophy triumphs. Apart from this plethora of Welshmen there were other names to conjure with – Osbaldestin, Hudson, Brown, Miller, Kenny, Bradbury, Dalton, Middleton, Feetham – a glorious company.

When Risman returned from the 1932 tour he was entrusted with Salford's goal-kicking and proceeded to kick exactly 100 goals for the club in 1932-33 beating the record of 82 set in 1906-07 by the wonderful James Lomas, captain of the first touring team to Australasia in 1910. The following season Risman extended the record to 116 goals. Fifteen tries brought his points total to 277 which exceeded the record set by Lomas in 1906-07 by eleven points. Risman's best scoring feats in a match were 32 points against Bramley in 1933 and against Broughton Rangers in 1940 – both comprised of 13 goals and two tries. Gus place-kicked with his right foot but favoured the left when drop-kicking. By the time he played his farewell game for Salford against Rochdale Hornets on March 23rd, 1946 his scoring contribution to the club amounted to 143 tries, 789 goals and 2,007 points, records that were to remain intact for thirty years until another magic dragon in the shape of David Watkins caused the record books to be rewritten. Gus' finale at Salford took place two days after his 35th birthday. Anyone predicting that there were another 1,650 points waiting for the evergreen Gus to post would have been laughed to scorn.

Salford won the Lancashire Cup three times in succession in 1934, 1935 and 1936 defeating great rivals Wigan in each final. The scores became progressively closer – 21-12, 15-7 and 5-2 before Wigan eventually got the better of the men from Weaste in the final of 1938 when Sullivan's five goals resulted in a 10-8 victory. Risman kicked goals in all four of these finals including six in 1934. The day after the Lancashire Cup Final of 1934 (Oct 20th) Salford were playing in Paris and defeating the locals 51-36 after embarking on the first tour of France by a British club side. Six games were played and won at Paris, Lyons-Villeurbanne, Beziers, Albi, Perpignan and Villeneuve. Gus played in four of the games, collecting 25 goals and two tries, whilst "Toddy Toddlers" collected a new sobriquet – "Les Diables Rouges", "The Red Devils", a nick-name retained to this day.

In the ten seasons from the time Gus arrived at the Willows until the outbreak of war Salford never finished lower than ninth in the league and made the top four play-offs on six occasions. They topped the league in 1932-33, 1933-34, 1936-37 and 1938-39, winning the Lancashire League in each of those seasons and in 1934-35. Gus helped the club to Championship Finals in 1933, 1934, 1937 and 1939, only one of which (1934 to Wigan) was lost. In the final of 1933 Gus kicked three goals in the 15-5 defeat of Swinton. Four years later at Central Park Warrington appeared to have put paid to Salford's Championship bid when hooker Dave Cotton scored a try to give the "Wire" an 11-8 lead, at which point Risman's four penalty goals seemed to have been kicked in vain. The Red Devils were not done with, however, and with five minutes left on the clock Barney Hudson scored a try to equalise. As in many another hard-fought encounter everything depended on Risman's boot. Gus' nerve was unaffected and his aim true and the Championship went to Salford on a 13-11 verdict. The Championship Final of 1939 took place at Maine Road, Manchester and a record Rugby League crowd of 69,504 saw Salford edge out Castleford 8-6. Both sides scored two tries but Gus' first-half penalty was the only goal landed and effectively won the title.

The Rugby League Challenge Cup is always regarded as the blue ribbon of this uncompromising and demanding sport and it was the only trophy that had eluded "The Red Devils" of Lance Todd's vintage. Finally in 1938 they fought their way to the twin towers of Wembley conceding only five points *en route*. Their opponents were Alec Troup's Barrow and Risman, from stand-off, led a Salford side containing eight Welshmen – four backs and four forwards. The game proved to be a close but largely unspectacular affair and with a minute to go was dead-locked at 4-4. Barrow had drawn first blood with a penalty after nine minutes

Wembley 1938. Three happy Welshmen.
Harold Watkin Thomas (ex-Neath and Wales R.U.) and Risman hoist the Trophy, inadvertently framing

which Risman had cancelled out with a similar score after 22 minutes. Just before half-time Gus struck again when Salford heeled from a scrum in the Barrow "25" and Watkins served him standing deep. Gus appeared to be about to launch his three-quarters but instead swung his left boot and effortlessly dropped as sweet a goal as could be imagined. Twenty-one minutes into the second-half the Barrow scrum-half Billy Little took a leaf out of the gospel according to Gus to drop an equalising goal – also with his left foot and also from a scrum around the "25". Although the match was not a spell-binder Risman was the one man who rose to the occasion. Reports say he was *"quite the most dangerous man on the field"*, *"a leader who was able to do things"*, *"whose strength at half was considerable"*. If there had been a Lance Todd Trophy in 1938 Risman would have been the clear winner. Just as it seemed that the first try-less Wembley final was to materialise, Salford's full-back Osbaldestin kicked through and Barrow began a passing movement which broke down. Salford's centre, Albert Gear, formerly of Newport and Torquay, took the ball through at his feet and beat three Barrow defenders to the touchdown. Risman failed to convert but it hardly mattered as his kick was the last act of the match. Don Bradman presented the Cup to Gus, who thus became the first and only Salford captain to lift the trophy.

The following year Salford battled through to Wembley again, this time conceding no tries and only four points on their way. There was to be no repeat victory for the Red Devils on this occasion, however, as Halifax won comfortably by 20-3. Gus, this time playing at centre, scored Salford's only try. Despite defeat in both the Challenge Cup and Lancashire Cup Finals 1938-39 had been a great season for Gus and his Red Devils, who had topped the league suffering only seven defeats in 40 matches, had taken the Rugby League Championship and lifted the Lancashire League title. For the only time in his career Gus finished as the League's leading scorer with 267 points – seven more than the maestro himself, Jim Sullivan.

Salford closed down in 1941 for the duration of the war and Gus played his Rugby League as a guest player for Leeds, Bradford Northern and Dewsbury. He also made two appearances for Hunslet. Whilst guesting for Bradford Northern in 1940-41 he played in their Yorkshire Cup Final victory over Dewsbury and was stand-off in both legs of their Championship Final victory over Wigan compiling three tries in the two games. The following season he appeared in the Challenge Cup Final at Odsal in the blue and amber of Leeds when Halifax were vanquished 15-10 – some compensation for Wembley 1939. Welshmen scored all Leeds points with Alan Edwards (2) and Oliver Morris scoring tries and Risman contributing three goals. A few weeks earlier he and four other Salford backs had assisted Dewsbury to overcome Bradford Northern 13-0 in the Emergency League Championship Final. His war-time rugby was not, of course, confined to the League variety for he proved his greatness in the

Union game, leading his country in internationals (Services) at Gloucester and Cardiff when his team-mates included such luminaries of
Welsh Union as Wilf Wooller, Haydn Tanner and Bleddyn Williams.

On returning from the 1946 Tour Risman opened up a new chapter
in his rugby odyssey by taking over as player-manager at Workington
Town. Cumberland already had a long tradition for producing Rugby
League players but despite providing a county team to rival Yorkshire
and Lancashire it had never possessed a professional club until Workington Town entered the League in 1945-46, when they finished a creditable
19th in the Championship.

When Risman took over no-one would have imagined that the "old
man" would play another eight full seasons and 301 matches for the
infant club. Still less would they have believed that within five years of
Risman's arrival Town would be wearing the mantle of Rugby League
Champions and that within six years the Rugby League Challenge Cup
would be winging its way from Wembley to Workington. The records
show that Risman wrought these miracles.

In his time at Workington Gus operated mostly from the full-back
position so his career had come full circle. In fact it appeared to be going
round and round and round. There were those who thought he would go
on for ever. By the end of his first season Gus had lifted the club to
eleventh position and 1947-48 saw the lusty infant just denied a place in
the top four. That season Gus set club records of 96 goals and 198 points
but he was only just beginning! He was to extend both records in 1949-
50, 1950-51 and in 1953-54. No wonder he became known as the "Peter
Pan of Rugby League".

By 1950-51 Gus had assembled and moulded a team capable of
beating the very best. Cumbrians, Scots, Lancastrians and Australians
helped to put Workington Town firmly on the Rugby League map. There
was even a fellow Welshman in the side – stand-off John Thomas from
Crynant. The club finished in third place and qualified for a crack at
Wigan in the Championship semi-final. Overcoming the loss of loose-
forward Billy Ivison through injury in the first half, Workington stunned
the Wigan crowd and the Rugby League world at large by grinding out
an 8-5 victory and so qualified to meet Warrington in the final at Maine
Road where over 61,000 fans assembled to watch Bevan, Bath, Helme and
company put the Cumbrian upstarts in their place. At the interval it
seemed that what was expected would come to pass for despite losing
winger Albert Johnson with a broken leg in the opening minutes Warrington played superbly to lead 8-3. The second half, however, was all
Workington Town. Gus converted an Eppie Gibson try to level the scores
and shortly afterwards kicked a penalty to put his side in the lead for the
first time and the the flood-gates opened as Town swept to a 26-11
victory. Gus received the Championship trophy – eighteen years after
participating in his first Championship Final.

The following season Town relinquished their hold on the Championship finishing in eighth position but more than atoned by reaching the Challenge Cup Final. It was Gus' third Wembley Final and at 41 he became the oldest player to appear there. Town's opponents were Featherstone Rovers. The attendance of 73,000 – about twice the population of Workington and Featherstone combined – was the largest before which Gus ever appeared. From the moment that Risman kicked a forty yard penalty at Featherstone's first play-the-ball the Cup was destined to be lifted by Gus. Although Rovers gave the Cumbrians some very anxious moments and clawed their way back to 7-7 they were never able to snatch the lead. In the 60th minute Rovers' hour was up and disaster struck. Their prop, Jack Daly – revered by his fellow Irishmen for scoring the try against Wales that gave Ireland the Triple Crown in 1948 – dummied his way cleverly past two Town defenders into the Workington "25" only to throw a suicidal pass which was summarily intercepted by winger Johnny Lawrenson who did not stop until he touched down under the posts at the other end of the pitch. It was the killer blow. Risman converted with his third goal and Town won 18-10. Gus accepted the Cup from Anthony Eden – fourteen years after he had first lifted it, another record to add to his list. In his three Wembley Finals he had played in three different positions and he had scored in each.

Gus continued to inspire his team until 1954. He remained a master of tactics and his kicking seemed to become even deadlier. In his final season at Workington (1953-54) he led his team to the Championship semi-finals once more, playing in all 45 matches that Town contested, an amazing accomplishment for a 43 year-old. Moreover, he only failed to score in one match and kicked more goals (138) and scored more points (294) than he had ever done before in a single season. The man appeared indestructible – if not irreplaceable.

Following a dispute over selection matters Gus resigned his post and joined Batley, kicking seven goals on his debut against Doncaster. His last appearance was as Batley's full-back in a local derby against Dewsbury at Mount Pleasant on December 27th, 1954, his three goals contributing much to a 12-5 victory.

After finishing playing Gus went back to Salford as manager in February 1955 and later held managerial posts at Oldham and Bradford Northern.

His contribution to the game went even further for his two sons Bev and John followed in his footsteps and there has been a Risman playing professionally almost continuously since 1929. Bev, of course, played for England and the British Lions at Union, before becoming an outstanding full-back and goal-kicker with Leigh and Leeds. He also emulated his father by attaining the captaincy of Great Britain whilst his brother John began his career at Gus' old club Workington and went on to play for Cumberland and Wales.

Players like Gus Risman come along once in a life-time. Thankfully Gus' career seemed to last a life-time.

GUS RISMAN'S PLAYING RECORD FOR SALFORD

	GAMES	TRIES	GOALS	POINTS
1929-30	42	3	—	9
1930-31	41	2	4	14
1931-32	39	16	13	74
1932-33	34	16	100	248
1933-34	35	15	116	277
1934-35	35	10	89	208
1935-36	39	17	92	235
1936-37	35	16	66	180
1937-38	33	17	96	243
1938-39	47	18	104	262
1939-40	27	11	81	195
1940-41	2	—	—	—
1945-46	18	2	28	62
TOTALS	427	143	789	2,007

Note: These figures do not include Salford's tour of France in 1934.

GUS RISMAN'S PLAYING RECORD FOR WORKINGTON TOWN

	GAMES	TRIES	GOALS	POINTS
1946-47	32	6	46	110
1947-48	43	2	96	198
1948-49	31	2	65	136
1949-50	42	4	104	220
1950-51	38	7	108	237
1951-52	37	1	87	177
1952-53	33	5	73	161
1953-54	45	6	138	294
TOTALS	301	33	717	1,533

All first-class matches:

	873	232	1,678	4,052

Chapter 4

Wigan Welsh – Wizards and Wings
(Bert Jenkins, Johnny Thomas, Danny Hurcombe, Johnny Ring, Jack Morley)

No northern club has more profitably pillaged the Welsh Rugby Union community down the years than Wigan and the Central Park club has provided more players to the Welsh RL team than any other. The roll of honour of Wigan's Welshmen is long and illustrious and to do justice to them all would require a complete volume in itself. The five players portrayed in this chapter are among the very greatest of all Wigan's Welsh wonders.

BERT JENKINS & JOHNNY THOMAS

The careers of Bert Jenkins and Johnny Thomas ran so remarkably parallel that their stories are essentially the same. Both were born in 1884, Jenkins in Troedyrhiw and Thomas in Aberkenfig and both made their debuts for Wigan in December 1904. Neither made a great impression on their first appearances. Jenkins first wore the cherry and white against Runcorn on December 9th, 1904, performed indifferently and caught a cold which persisted for several weeks. Nineteen days later Thomas stepped forth at Central Park against Broughton Rangers and produced a performance which persuaded the Wigan directorate that he needed to learn the game in the reserves for a while. Both went on to establish themselves as truly great players. Thomas played his last game for Wigan in April 1920, Jenkins five months later.

The pair saw Wigan transformed from a nondescript, parochial club into a highly successful, pot-winning concern drawing its playing members from all corners of the rugby-playing world. None of the major trophies had found their way to Central Park before 1905 when the club took the Lancashire Cup in its inaugural season. In the years 1905-14, however, everything changed as Wigan contested a dozen major finals and won the Lancashire League Championship six times in the last seven seasons before the Great War brought competitive rugby to an end – they were runners-up in the remaining season (1909-10). Johnny Thomas took his place at half-back in all twelve of those finals whilst Jenkins missed only two because of injury.

Thomas Bertram Jenkins was the first to arrive at Central Park signing for the Wigan club on December 8th, 1904. He had begun his playing career with his village team of Troedyrhiw as a half-back before

Bert Jenkins

progressing to Mountain Ash where his centre play would surely have ultimately earned him an amateur cap had Wigan not spirited him away. The era in which Jenkins flourished produced some of the finest centre-three-quarters the sport has ever known. Harold Wagstaff, the great dictator and innovator at Huddersfield; Billy Batten of Hunslet, spectacular, powerful and charismatic; and James Lomas of Salford, ubiquitous and unyielding, a man who could dominate a game from start to finish. Jenkins ranks alongside that Holy Trinity as a sacred centre. A powerful and punishing tackler, Jenkins was the most correct centre of his day in terms of style. He did everything as the text-book laid down. His orthodoxy was striking and it was no handicap to him at Wigan where there were so many brilliantly unorthodox performers. His precise, unselfish skills brought out the best in his sometimes wayward colleagues. Jenkins was perhaps most noted for his sublime partnership with "Gentleman Jim" Leytham, arguably the finest winger of the Edwardian era. This left-wing combination, the pair scoring well over 300 tries together, was the marvel of the Northern Union for eight seasons until Leytham was forced to retire in 1912. Each knew exactly what the other was about and Leytham could be sure that Jenkins would never give him a bad ball. Jenkins played no small part in Leytham's topping the try-scoring charts in 1906, 1908 and 1910 and his own tally of almost 200 tries for the club is a potent reminder that he was no slouch at finding the try-line too.

In front of Jenkins was Johnny Thomas feeding him the ammunition to fire Leytham. Thomas, the archetypal Welsh fly-half, had commenced his senior rugby as a full-back with Maesteg and graduated to scrum-half and had played Welsh trials in both those positions. In 1904 he had been persuaded by Cecil Biggs, the Cardiff International and captain, to play for that famous club. Thomas duly turned out against Llanelli, displaying his burgeoning virtuosity and promptly signed for Wigan for a consideration of £200. "Dinny" Campbell, the Australian centre, who played for Leeds and was a contemporary of Johnny, wrote:

> *"Thomas was stockily built, with plenty of 'nip' off the mark. He flashed through the opposition in a way that told of his remarkably quick football brain. His perfect positional play, and the command he always had over every situation, stamped him as a footballer of outstanding ability. He was a team man, he got his backs going with such smoothness and precision that football looked easy, his defence was just as sound as his attack, and his kicking was a delight".*

Thomas was certainly a fine goal-kicker and landed close on 500 goals in his first-class career. That total would have been a great deal larger had it not been Wigan's good fortune to field fine kickers such as Jack "Safety-pin" Mason and Jim Leytham (whose talents knew no bounds) in his earlier days at the club. Johnny's best performances with

Johnny Thomas

the boot for Wigan comprised of eleven goals against Runcorn on January 30th, 1915, a feat which had been preceded by three weeks by a ten goal haul against Broughton Rangers. Another tally of ten was recorded against Coventry on November 20th, 1912. In 1912-13 he eclipsed Leytham's club record of 71 goals (1908-09) by landing 82 and also topped the league's scoring charts by claiming 198 points. A season later he broke his own record by kicking 83 goals.

Undoubtedly Thomas' finest kicking occurred in his second international for Wales. The game, at Tonypandy on Easter Monday 1908, produced a remarkable 35-18 victory over England with Wales recovering strongly after trailing 18-15 at half-time. Thomas landed seven goals out of seven attempts in an immaculate exhibition of his art. Only Paul Woods, the Widnes scrum-half, has equalled this feat for Wales – against France in 1978. Bert Jenkins had reason to be pleased with his work in that match too as he scored a brace of tries and put his winger Llewellyn Treharne in for a couple. Treharne was also a Wigan player, who had previously assisted Merthyr and Penygraig.

Just as their club football careers went hand in glove so too did the international experiences of Thomas and Jenkins. Both made their debuts for Wales on New Year's Day, 1908 when the Welsh played their inaugural professional international beating New Zealand 9-8 at Aberdare. Wales played eleven internationals in the period 1908-14 and only Bert Jenkins figured in them all, a remarkable achievement. His Welsh appearances yielded him four tries, all against England. Johnny Thomas won eight Welsh caps despite fierce competition for the stand-off position from the likes of Jim Davies and Johnny Rogers. Thomas kicked 17 goals from Wales but never scored a try. Both rose to the captaincy of Wales, Jenkins attaining the honour first.

Both also won the higher distinction of captaining test teams. Jenkins holds an immutable place in the game's annals as captain of the first Northern Union test team to meet Australia in a drawn game at Park Royal, London on December 12th, 1908. Jenkins and Thomas played in all three tests in that first Ashes-winning series, although James Lomas took over the captaincy for the second and third tests. Johnny Thomas captained the test team in the first test of 1911 at Newcastle kicking two goals as his side went down to a 19-10 defeat by the Kangaroos. That was the last of his eight tests. Although Thomas had never managed to touch down for Wales he is perhaps unique in League history for having scored tries in six consecutive test matches. Thomas scored tries in each of the three tests against Australia in 1908-09, in the two tests down-under in 1910 and in the solitary New Zealand test of 1910.

Jenkins and Thomas had also figured in the first test match ever played when they lined up against New Zealand at Headingley on January 25th, 1908 when the British triumphed 14-6. Jim Leytham was Jenkins' winger on that historic occasion. Jenkins' test career was longer than Thomas' and embraced twelve matches ending at Auckland in 1914. The two toured together in 1910 with Jenkins making a second tour in 1914. The two great Welshmen also played together for Lancashire and in 1921 shared a benefit together with Dick Ramsdale, a local-born forward and colleague on the 1910 tour.

In domestic rugby 1908-09 was one of Wigan's most rewarding seasons. For the first time the club topped the league table losing only four of their 32 fixtures and playing a brand of open rugby that brought them almost 200 points more than their nearest rivals, Halifax. The three-quarter line scored no fewer than 131 tries with the Jenkins-Leytham wing contributing 61 and the Lance Todd-Joe Miller partnership 70. Also won for the first time was the Lancashire League and the county double was achieved when Oldham were defeated in the Lancashire Cup Final at Broughton. The game on a mud-bound pitch was an encounter of the closest kind with Oldham clinging to a 9-7 lead late into the proceedings. Wigan would certainly have been out of contention by that stage had it not been for some superb defence largely inspired by Jenkins but it was Thomas who decided the destination of the trophy. Breaking from his own half, he served his Kiwi centre Todd and followed up the latter's short kick, kicking on again at half-way to beat Oldham's international backs Llewellyn and Wood in a desperate race for the touch-down, thus enabling Wigan to finish winners by 10-9.

Oldham were also the victims in Wigan's first annexation of the Championship for later that season the Roughyeds were beaten 7-3 at Salford in the Championship Final. In the following two seasons, however, Oldham reversed the result and Wigan suffered the mortification of losing four consecutive Championship Finals as Huddersfield beat them in the finals of 1912 and 1913.

The one trophy that eluded the cherry and whites in 1908-09 was the Challenge Cup as Wakefield Trinity removed them at the semi-final stage. Jenkins and Thomas never did win that coveted medal as only once was the final to witness their skills and Broughton Rangers proved too strong winning 4-0 in 1911.

That aside, there were few disappointments for Jenkins and Thomas, purveyors of middle back perfection in Wigan's first golden age.

BERT JENKINS' PLAYING RECORD FOR WIGAN

	GAMES	TRIES	GOALS	POINTS
1904-05	8	1	—	3
1905-06	35	13	—	39
1906-07	31	23	—	69
1907-08	27	13	—	39
1908-09	41	24	—	72
1909-10	33	10	—	30
1910-11	35	18	—	54
1911-12	36	17	—	51
1912-13	40	23	—	69
1913-14	37	22	—	66
1914-15	27	10	—	30
1918-19	9	—	—	—
1919-20	27	7	—	21
1920-21	3	—	—	—
TOTALS	389	181	—	543

All first-class matches:

	GAMES	TRIES	GOALS	POINTS
	451	218	—	654

JOHNNY THOMAS' PLAYING RECORD FOR WIGAN

	GAMES	TRIES	GOALS	POINTS
1904-05	17	2	—	6
1905-06	39	12	1	38
1906-07	33	12	4	44
1907-08	33	9	14	55
1908-09	40	13	42	123
1909-10	37	18	46	146
1910-11	33	11	36	105
1911-12	24	4	33	78
1912-13	41	8	82	188
1913-14	32	8	83	190
1914-15	38	5	77	169
1918-19	10	2	17	40
1919-20	11	2	5	16
TOTALS	388	106	440	1,198

All first-class matches:

	GAMES	TRIES	GOALS	POINTS
	428	120	484	1,328

DANNY HURCOMBE

There was not all that much of Danny Hurcombe, whose vital statistics in 1924 were reported to be 5' 7" and 10st 9lbs, but his talents were immense. There were those who thought that Hurcombe embodied all the skills of Thomas, Jenkins and Leytham in his small frame. He was a man who performed superlatively in practically every position in the back-line, an international at stand-off, centre and wing. There were also those who found him arrogant and testy. Harold Wagstaff once recalled how Johnny Thomas tended to stutter when he became excited. He would never have been able to say the same about the man who succeeded the tongue-tied Thomas as king-pin of the Wigan back division for Danny Hurcombe was as vitriolic with his tongue as he was venomous to all forms of defence. Hurcombe knew he was good and he liked other people to know it. Fortunately he could back up his words with deeds.

Hurcombe was a creative player of the first order, quick to exploit weakness in the opposition, blessed with tremendous acceleration off the mark and a fine distributor. He certainly did not suffer from claustrophobia and Houdini himself would have envied the way in which Hurcombe could work in small spaces. He had the most remarkable knack of being able to extricate himself from the tightest of situations wriggling and worming his way out of opponents' clutches when he seemed well and truly bottled up. For such a small man he was a dreadnought in defence, a fearless tackler who gave not a fig for reputations and he was often called upon to shackle a particularly dangerous opponent.

A native of Abersychan, Hurcombe was captain of Talywain when Wigan procured his signature on November 13th, 1919. He had also played for Cross Keys and Monmouthshire. Six days later he made his debut in an 11-0 defeat at Widnes. In the aftermath of the Great War Wigan were not the great side that they had previously been and at the season's end the club was half-way down the league in thirteenth position. Evidence that they would soon attain a place of eminence, however, glistened from their achievement of reaching the Northern Union Challenge Cup Final. Their opponents were Huddersfield whose pre-war stars were still burning bright. Wigan gave Wagstaff's Team of All the Talents a hard fight but went down 21-10 and it seemed that the Challenge Cup was destined never to rest at Central Park. Hurcombe played centre that day after barely a score of matches in his new code. Even more remarkably, he had already won selection for the 1920 tour of Australasia just a few months after his entry into the game. Hurcombe was one of eight Welshmen chosen to tour and surprisingly it was as a centre that he was chosen.

Hurcombe played alongside Wagstaff in the first and second tests in Australia which were both lost. It must have seemed strange to see the

Danny Hurcombe

dapper, little Hurcombe operating at centre to a winger the size of Jim Bacon of Leeds in those tests. Bacon, formerly of Pill Harriers, Cross Keys and the Welsh Guards, was a big, strong player even by modern standards. At his peak he weighed around 14 stones and he was an excellent sprinter. Certainly he had a physique more in keeping with a centre than Hurcombe. The pair actually played together as centres in the first test in New Zealand when Britain won 31-7.

The next time Hurcombe played test rugby was at Salford in the third test in 1922 when he was given the wing spot with the specific role of stopping the great Australian wing Cec Blinkhorn who had scored three tries in the first two tests and was clearly one of the Kangaroos' most potent threats. Hurcombe stuck to Blinkhorn like a limpet and the great man never looked like scoring as the British won a foul-weather match 6-0 to regain the Ashes.

In 1924 Hurcombe was selected for his second tour in the company of four of his team-mates in Jim Sullivan, Tommy Howley, Johnny Ring (all Welsh) and Jack Price. This time he went as first-choice stand-off and played in that position in two of the Australian tests, the Ashes being retained, and in the second New Zealand test. For the final New Zealand test and his own last test Hurcombe was back on the wing scoring his first and only test try as the British won 31-18 at Dunedin.

Hurcombe won seven caps for Wales as a League player scoring five tries in the process, twice registering two against England in 1923 – in February at Wigan and in October at Fartown. In his final three Welsh games he captained the side and bowed out with a try against New Zealand at Pontypridd in 1926. Despite his frequent clashes with authority he was also awarded the captaincy in his two internationals for Other Nationalities against England in 1924 and 1926.

Whilst Hurcombe was a Wigan player the club won four Lancashire League Championships, the Rugby League Championship in 1922 (Hurcombe did not play in the final) and at long last the Challenge Cup in 1924 when Hurcombe partnered Sid Jerram at half-back in a 21-4 victory over Oldham. Of the Wigan backs that historic day only the South African master-wing Attie Van Heerden was not from the valleys. An even more graphic reminder of just how fruitful South Wales was to Wigan's recruitment strategy was the composition of the team that defeated Leigh 20-2 in the Lancashire Cup Final of 1922. On that occasion the back division read Sullivan, Ring, Howley, Shea, Hurcombe, Owens and Jerram – each a Welsh cap, present or future. Of the pack Wilf Hodder, Fred Roffey, Percy Coldrick and Tom Woods were also Welsh Internationals, although the latter was an Englishman with five England RU caps to his credit. Woods had been a playing colleague of Hodder at Pontypool when the pair came north in 1921. Thus only two of the thirteen Wigan players in that final had not been recruited from South Wales.

Syd Jerram – ex Swansea half-back.
Signed for Wigan in 1913 for £180.

Between the wars Wigan employed many of their Welsh players as ground staff at Central Park where they did odd jobs such as boot-repairing. They were paid a small wage in addition to their match fees.

Danny Hurcombe turned out for Wigan for the last time in a home game against Wakefield Trinity on January 23rd, 1926. He later played with Halifax and Leigh before finishing his career at Keighley where he played his final game on October 1st, 1932 in a 28-5 victory over Rochdale Hornets.

Had Hurcombe been a more malleable personality and played out his career with Wigan instead of wrangling with them and his subsequent less successful clubs, there is little doubt that his achievements would have been greater. His place in the pantheon of great players, high though it is, may have been unapproachable. He was not the first sportsman of genius to allow his personality to spite his talent.

DANNY HURCOMBE'S PLAYING RECORD FOR WIGAN

	GAMES	TRIES	GOALS	POINTS
1919-20	23	7	3	27
1920-21	25	6	—	18
1921-22	31	13	—	39
1922-23	38	15	—	45
1923-24	26	9	—	27
1924-25	32	15	—	45
1925-26	24	5	—	15
TOTALS	199	70	3	216

All first-class matches:

	317	97	18	327

JOHNNY RING

In the programme for the Gala Opening of the Welsh Rugby Union centenary year in 1980 Vivian Jenkins recalled how he had, as a nine-year-old, crawled through a hole in the fence of Aberavon's Mansel ground to see his first top-class club match. The year was 1920 and Jenkins wrote:

> *"My other outstanding memory of the match is Aberavon's right wing, a 'flyer' named Johnny Ring, who seemed to us youngsters the fastest thing on two legs we had ever seen. He at once became my first schoolboy hero . . . . . Not very long afterwards Johnny 'went north' . . . . . and it broke my heart".*

J. RING
WIGAN R.F.L.

Johnny Ring

Vivian Jenkins' heart was not the only one to be broken when Ring went north to Wigan for countless hardened professional rugby players suffered cardiac trouble trying to keep pace with the Aberavon Wizard and a myriad Lancashire schoolboys found a new idol to worship.

By the time Ring retired from the game in 1933 he had scored more tries than anyone else in the sport's history having during the 1930-31 season eclipsed Rosenfeld's previous record of 392 touchdowns. His final total of 418 tries was ample testimony to his right to be called the greatest winger of his era. Although he had many of the attributes which go to make up the ideal wing-man in terms of elusiveness and finishing skills, Johnny Ring's crowning glory was the sheer blistering pace that he was able to generate, often in runs covering the length of the field. There was simply no point in chasing Johnny Ring once he glimpsed day-light. His scoring feats were phenomenal, to the point where even Jim Leytham's mighty achievements were put into the shade. Ring had passed Leytham's club record of 258 tries within six seasons of his debut and it would take an ever greater winger, unimaginable though that may have seemed for those who saw him, in the shape of Billy Boston to wrest the record from him almost 40 years later.

Johnny Ring, a native of Port Talbot, was born on November 13th, 1900. His father Cornelius Ring, a champion sprinter in the Principality, certainly transmitted in good measure his athletic genes to his offspring. Progressing through Aberavon Harlequins to the senior Aberavon side, Johnny Ring soon made it clear that a try-scoring prodigy occupied the Wizards' wing. In the three seasons he played for the Wizards he raced in for no fewer than 196 tries, setting a club record of 76 in 1919-20. At the time Wales was full of excellent wingers and when Ring changed codes in 1922 he was the fourth capped winger to do so since competitive rugby had restarted after the war.

Both Welsh wingers of the 1920 team had gone north – Wickham Powell of Cardiff to Rochdale Hornets and Llanelli's Brinley Williams to Batley. Ring was capped in 1921 against England at Twickenham but lost his place in the following Scottish game to Llanelli's Frank Dafen Evans. Evans, a remarkably elusive player, brimful of resource and a devil of a man to tackle went north to Swinton a year before Ring with whom he was to tour the Antipodes in 1924. Evans became a test player and set his own try-scoring records at Swinton, where his aggregate of 197 tries (1921-31) remains unsurpassed.

Ring's solitary Union cap was certainly no true reflection of his ability for selectors of Welsh teams in the twenties were notoriously fickle. England won the Grand Slam that year with Wales being accounted for 18-3. Ring's try at the corner was the only one registered against England throughout the championship. The Welsh side contained Newport's Jerry Shea, a wayward but spasmodically brilliant centre, and Pontypool's sterling forward Wilf Hodder both of whom

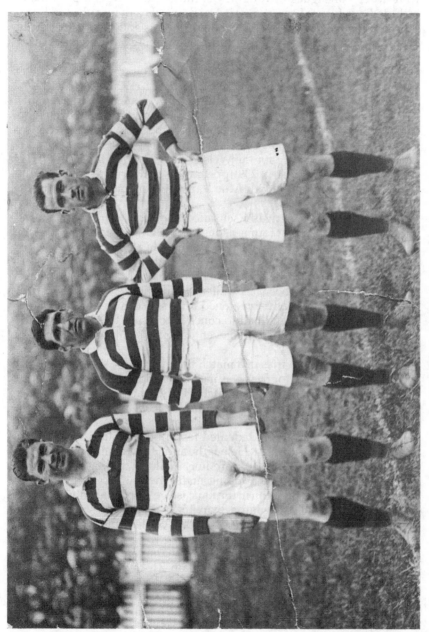

Three Great Wigan Welsh.
Jim Sullivan, Jerry Shea, and Johnny Ring.

were to be colleagues of Ring at Central Park. Hodder's pack-mates included two future League men in Dai Edwards (Glynneath) and Edgar Morgan (Llanelli) who joined Rochdale Hornets and Hull respectively. In the English pack was another future team-mate of Ring in the shape of Tom Woods.

Wigan paid Ring £800 to surrender his amateur status, the winger making his debut against Salford on August 26th, 1922. Ring's left-wing partnership with Tommy Howley, the ex-Ebbw Vale man, was reminiscent of the old, hallowed Jenkins-Leytham act and produced even more tries. Within six months of Ring throwing in his lot with Wigan he was joined at Central Park by his old Aberavon centre partner Tommy Parker who had tired of waiting for the Welsh selectors to see the light. Parker scored 114 tries for Wigan in 239 appearances and formed a potent right-wing combination firstly with Attie Van Heerden and latterly with the classy Kiwi, Lou Brown.

From the start Ring was a sensation and scoring tries was second nature to him. In his first four seasons his try tallies were 44, 49, 54, and 63 and he was the League's top try-scorer in each. The 63 tries Ring scored in 1925-26 remains the biggest bag by any British winger in the game's history. Sixty-two of those tries were plundered for his club, the nearest approach to which has been 59 by Ellery Hanley in 1986-87. Not even the fabulous Boston has really threatened Ring's record season. In 1926-27 Johnny scored 49 tries and had to concede top spot to Alf Ellaby of St. Helens. Ellaby was the man who eventually passed Johnny's record of 418 tries.

Ring scored seven tries in a match three times for Wigan and twice scored six. His hunger for tries was insatiable and throughout his career he averaged more than a try per match. He did not merely run in tries in the "easy" fixtures but had some outstanding feats to his credit when the chips were really down. In 1925-26, for example, he scored hat-tricks in two major finals – an unprededented feat. In the Championship Final victory over Warrington at St. Helens, he and Howley accounted for five of their side's six tries in a 22-10 score-line. Earlier in the season, however, Johnny was reported to be hopping mad when he scored all three of Wigan's tries against Swinton in the Lancashire Cup Final only to pick up a runners-up medal as Swinton won 15-11, thanks to some cardinal errors committed on the other wing by Van Heerden who apparently had had a very late night.

In 1924 Wigan at last inscribed their name on the Rugby League Challenge Cup after overcoming Oldham 21-4 at Rochdale where a record crowd of 40,786 had assembled. In scenes reminiscent of the first F.A. Cup Final at Wembley, mounted police had to patrol the touch-lines because of encroachment by the spectators. Johnny Ring described his try thus:

"I scored the last try of the match for Wigan and nearly ran into a horse in doing it! The crowd was over the line and becoming more and more excited as the game drew to its close. Oldham were losing and some of their supporters were demonstrating on the goal-line. It became increasingly obvious that they would be reluctant to stand back when we came up again. Obtaining the ball, I headed for the line, but I was worried when I saw that they were determined to hold me back, so in sheer desperation I threw myself with the ball into the body of the crowd, right on top of an Oldham fan, flattening him as the try was scored."

Van Heeden actually had to run round a horse to score in that momentous match.

Ring was a member of the Wigan team which won the Cup in 1929 when Wembley was used for the first time. It was one of the few big matches in which Ring failed to get onto the score-sheet but he was no doubt happy with his second winners' medal. Ring's career at Wigan ended on Boxing Day, 1931 in a local derby with St. Helens. After falling out with Wigan, who would not grant him a testimonial, Ring moved to Rochdale Hornets on January 22nd, 1932. Just over a year later he retired having made 26 appearances as a Hornet during which he added a dozen tries to his mammoth haul.

Despite his prolific scoring Johnny Ring found it difficult to win the approval of the international selectors. There were, of course, lots of good wingers about, some of whom were undoubtedly inferior as try-scoring machines but whose defensive capabilities were perhaps superior. The avalanche of tries emanating from his skills did not win him a Welsh cap until 1925 when both he and Frank Evans scored twice in a 27-22 defeat by England. Six appearances for Wales brought Ring five tries and rebuked the selectors' folly.

His test career was decidedly short consisting of the first test in Australia in 1924 and the first test against New Zealand at Wigan in 1926 both of which ended in victories for the British. Unfortunately for Johnny on the 1924 tour, on which he was the leading try-getter with 23 in only 17 games, he had inadvertently "done a Hurcombe" and offended authority. His offence, hardly heinous, had been to miss a train along with Warrington's Billy Cunliffe. The two had been more interested in eating an impromptu meal than in getting to the station in time. As a result they were both banned from future tours. The selectors relented only once by selecting the pair for the test at Wigan in 1926. The only parties to benefit from Ring's international exile were Great Britain's adversaries.

JOHNNY RING'S PLAYING RECORD FOR WIGAN

	GAMES	TRIES	GOALS	POINTS
1922-23	41	44	1	134
1923-24	40	48	1	146
1924-25	33	52	—	156
1925-26	37	62	—	186
1926-27	38	48	—	144
1927-28	26	18	—	54
1928-29	37	32	—	96
1929-30	26	26	1	80
1930-31	40	33	—	99
1931-32	12	8	—	24
TOTALS	330	371	3	1,119

All first-class matches:

	GAMES	TRIES	GOALS	POINTS
	388	418	3	1,260

JACK MORLEY

The money Jack Morely received for turning professional – reported as £500 – helped him to qualify as a dental surgeon. A legion of bewildered opposing wing-men wished fervently that he had stuck to pulling out teeth instead of making them look like fools for Morley had a peculiar aptitude for pulling games out of the fire with outrageous and improbable tries.

His capacity for try-scoring was well known before he signed for Wigan on August 29th, 1932, a month after his 23rd birthday. He came into Rugby League with the reputation of being one of Wales' greatest ever wing-men and he was the darling of the Welsh rugby-watching public. His renown had been well earned for he was indeed an exceptionally gifted Union player. Born in Newport on July 28th, 1909 he had attended Newport Municipal Secondary School from where he had won Schools caps in 1926-27 against Yorkshire Schools and France. Morley joined Newport aged eighteen and immediately made his mark. He had to be good to replace George Andrews, the five times capped international, who had gone north to join Leeds. His first season at Rodney Parade brought him 29 tries and in the five campaigns he served Newport his try tally was 115 from 151 appearances. In his last season with the black and ambers (1931-32) Morley was accorded the captaincy becoming the youngest man to fill the position for the club.

Jack Morley

Like Johnny Ring, Morley won his first Welsh cap in a defeat at Twickenham when Wales were beaten 8-3 on January 19th, 1929. Morley was only nineteen-and-a-half but was already being hailed as a great player. Also like Ring, Morley scored Wales' only try on his international debut, a startling weaving and dodging manoeuvre from outside the English "25", but unlike Ring he retained the selectors' confidence and went on to play 14 games for Wales. When Wales won the international championship in 1931 Morley scintillated in scoring four tries in four outings failing to touch down only against France at Swansea.

The most memorable try that Morley scored, however, in his amateur days was unquestionably for the British Isles against New Zealand in the first test at Dunedin on June 21st, 1930. The Lions had never won a test in New Zealand and on a really foul, wet and miserable day in Dunedin with the scores locked at 3-3 and time almost up it looked as if nothing would ever change. The All Blacks were in fact pressing inside the Lions' "25" when Llanelli's Ivor Jones snapped up a loose ball and darted into open space. He only had 85 yards to go! The All Blacks had been taken completely unawares and only the redoubtable George Nepia barred Jones' path to glory. Suddenly Jones had company in the flying Morley and so committed the great Maori to the tackle leaving the Newport winger to scorch half the length of the pitch to score at the corner. The Lions had beaten the All Blacks and Morley's niche in Union history was assured.

Fourteen Welsh caps and three for the Lions indicated to Wigan fans that the club had bought something special. Morley needed to be something special for his act was to follow Johnny Ring, not to mention Van Heerden and Lou Brown of recent vintage and all those earlier Wigan wonder wings. Morley did not let the fans down and entertained them royally right up to the outbreak of war.

Unlike Ring, Jack Morley was a right winger and at 5' 7" stood four inches shorter than his illustrious predecessor although the two weighed much the same at around 11 $1/_2$ stones. Whilst Morley was decidedly quick he did not rely upon sheer speed to the same extent as Johnny Ring to get him to the goal-line. Morley was marvellously unorthodox in his play and found all manner of means to torment the opposition. Those who saw Morley at his best say there has never been a player who could swerve so deceptively as this little, round-shouldered winger. His ability to circumnavigate defenders near the touch-line was simply astounding. Even when a tackler thought there was no space for Morley to utilise he would find some and there he was – gone! Acceleration, change of pace, elusiveness, unpredictability – Morley had the lot plus a sixth sense in backing up. He would often score by popping up in the most unexpected place in a movement and once clear he would gallop away from the opposition devouring the ground with his own short-stepping style.

His first season at Central Park yielded him 47 tries and he finished

Central Park, April 20th, 1929.

A Welsh version of Spot-the-ball. Jim Sullivan and Johnny Ring seem to be at cross purposes whilst George Andrews (ex-Newport & Wales R.U.) tries to keep his balance. His Leeds team-mate, Australian Jeff Moores seems to be synchronising with Ring!

second in the try-scoring charts to Leeds' great Australian winger, Eric Harris. His first three seasons brought Morley 140 touchdowns in all matches. Morley emulated Ring only once (1934-35) in respect of finishing as the League's leading try-scorer but the ex-Newport man never had a centre partner as reliable as Tommy Howley and consequently had to make much of his own luck.

Within three months of his first league match Morley was capped for Wales against England at Headingley scoring a try in a 14-13 defeat. In five appearances for Wales he scored five tries and failed to score only in his final game, a 17-14 victory over the English at Craven Park, Hull when Wales clinched the 1935-36 international championship. In late December 1933 he had the novel experience of scoring tries on successive days for Wales (at Wembley) and England (in Paris) against Australia, games in which the Australians rattled up 114 points in overwhelming victories.

In 1936 Morley won selection for the Great Britain touring team to Australasia along with his club colleague and centre, Gwynne Davies. Davies had been the other Welsh winger on Morley's debut as a Union International and had won three caps. He was the nephew of Johnny Thomas. The British won both the Australian and New Zealand series but Morley appeared in only the first test against Australia which was lost. His form on tour had not quite lived up to his club form and certainly did not touch that which he displayed in scoring five tries in the two tour trials.

Surprisingly Morley only played one more test and that was in 1937 when his try-scoring touch seemed to have deserted him for he scored only eleven tries that season. This second and final experience of test match rugby was gained in the first test against Australia at Leeds when a closely contested encounter resulted in a 5-4 victory for the British. After the 1937 series Morley had no chance to play test football as there were no more tests for nine years.

Although Wigan were still a powerful and repected team whilst Morley played only two trophies were won during his time at Central Park. The Championship was lifted in 1933-34 after Wigan had finished second to Salford in the table. Two tries in the play-offs by Morley were crucial factors in the cherry and whites' success. In the semi-final Wigan were trailing 10-2 to Leeds at Central Park with only fifteen minutes remaining and 27,000 people were convinced the Loiners were booked for the final. Wigan Welsh then took a hand and a try from George Bennett and two goals from Sullivan had the crowd in palpitations as Leeds were reduced to a one point lead with six minutes to go. Cometh the hour, cometh the man. In this case the man was Jack Morley and the try he scored could hardly have been more controversial. Bill Targett, the Wigan prop, suddenly began a dribble from centre-field and headed for the Leeds' goal-posts. Full-back Jim Brough was by-passed *en route* and a final stab of Targett's boot sent the ball bouncing mischievously in the shadows of the goal. Morley, inspired by that uncanny urge to be in the right place, had followed Targett's rush but Stanley Smith, the Leeds test winger, got there first and took the ball one-handed. Unfortunately for Smith he was on a collision course with the goal-post and was forced to lever himself off the upright. At that precise moment Morely clattered into him and the pair fell in an undignified heap below the bar where the two simultaneously touched the ball down and a try was awarded amid much consternation. Wigan thus qualified to meet Salford in the final at Warrington by virtue of an improbable 14-10 victory. The chance that Wigan might beat Salford was also considered highly improbable. The Red Devils had lost only six league fixtures whereas Wigan had lost twice as many. On the day the forecasts were all proved wrong. Wigan led five-nil when Morley struck the killing blow just before half-time. This time there was no controversy over the try's validity. It was merely one of Morley's more characteristic efforts as he shook off the Salford defence in a flying dash over half the length of the pitch. Wigan finally won 15-3. It was one of the few occasions in the 1930s when they managed to get the better of "Toddy's Toddlers" in a big match. Morley was in three Wigan teams to suffer defeat against Salford in three successive Lancashire Cup Finals (1934-36) but finally picked up a winners' medal in 1938 when five goals from Sullivan's infallible foot took Wigan to a 10-7 triumph over Risman's men.

Whenever arguments rage over great wingmen there is no doubt that the name of Jack Morley will be to the fore. Certainly he will never be forgotten at Newport or Wigan, two clubs which have seen more than their fair share of *nonpareils* in the position.

JACK MORLEY'S PLAYING RECORD FOR WIGAN

	GAMES	TRIES	GOALS	POINTS
1932-33	42	47	—	141
1933-34	40	41	1	125
1934-35	42	48	1	146
1935-36	42	22	—'	66
1936-37	36	20	—	60
1937-38	34	11	—	33
1938-39	47	27	—	81
1939-40	10	5	—	15
TOTALS	293	221	2	667

All first-class matches:

	GAMES	TRIES	GOALS	POINTS
	310	238	2	718

Chapter 5

Garfield Owen
(Newport RU, Halifax RL, Keighley RL)

If anyone could thread a camel through the eye of a needle there is a good chance that it would be Garfield Owen. When it came to projecting missiles of various shapes and sizes into their ordained places Garfield Owen was the man for the job. Fast bowler for Welsh Secondary schools, schoolboy discus champion of Wales, senior Welsh javelin champion – he missed a place in the Empire Games at Vancouver in 1950 by six inches – and a very fine golfer, threading camels through needles would appear to be well within his scope!

In view of his remarkable prowess in these varied sporting endeavours it is perhaps not too surprising that Owen should also be a gifted rugby player and a past master in his own particular art, that of kicking from hand or ground. As a full-back in either code Garfield Owen stands comparison with the very best, a man whose dependability and sureness engendered absolute confidence in those with whom he played. When it came to the try-saving tackle, the gathering of the most tantalising kick or the crucial goal attempt Owen's team-mates knew whom to trust. As a full-back and goal-kicker he was as safe as houses and epitomised the old-fashioned virtues deemed necessary in a top-class last line of defence. Full-back play under both League and Union laws during the last few decades has undergone radical changes to the extent that far from being the last line of defence the practitioner is now regarded in many ways as the first line of attack. It is fair to say that Garfield Owen represented one of the last and finest exponents of the old school of full-back play.

It was not always thus, however, for Garfield started his rugby career as a hooker at Cowbridge Grammar School but his mother quickly decided that no son of hers was going to be a hooker when he returned home with his jersey ripped. He was ordered not to go near any more scrums and from then on he played in the middle backs. It would have been hard for Owen not to have become a rugby player. Born in Llanharan, roughly equidistant from Bridgend and Cardiff, on March 20th, 1932 he sprang from the classical background of Welsh rugby players. His father, Jim, was a miner and had been captain of Llanharan RU club and Garfield David Owen was the culmination of several generations of family involvement in the club.

Moving from Dolau Elementary School to that bastion of the Union game, Cowbridge Grammar School, Garfield fell under the spell of the headmaster, Idwal Rees, who had been capped 14 times for Wales as a

A Cartoonist's view of Garfield Owen's signing.

Garfield Owen

three-quarter and risen to the captaincy. Mr. Rees was a great influence on the young Owen especially with regard to perfecting his place-kicking technique. Garfield always followed the head's advice which decreed that once the ball was placed the kicker should never on any account take his eyes off it. His assertion that the goal-posts would not move hardly entertained the possibility of contradiction. The young full-back was instructed not to look up until he heard cheering, otherwise there was nothing to look up for. Characteristically photographs of Owen depicting his high right-footed follow-through always show his glance directed downward. For Owen the position of the left foot was crucial. It must always point directly goalward to allow the kicking foot to follow straight through. Although Garfield never toured down-under it used to be a standing joke at Halifax that he was digging his way there because of the great piles of turf he excavated in placing the ball for goal-kicks. His method was to place the ball proud of the ground always pointing forward to a greater or lesser degree. He was able to punt with either foot prodigiously – the reward for countless hours of practice as a boy.

At fifteen he played for the Welsh Army Cadets against their English counterparts and as a sixteen year-old schoolboy played for Maesteg under an assumed name when school fixtures allowed. National Service saw him stationed at Oswestry where he played for the Royal Artillery, Wrexham and North Wales. On leaving the Army Owen trained as a teacher at Shoreditch College and later at Carnegie. It was whilst home on holiday that he got his first taste of big rugby in 1954. In a spell of playing about ten games during the course of a fortnight he received a telephone call asking him to play for Newport against the Barbarians on Easter Tuesday which was the following day. As he had just played for Maesteg that afternoon he politely suggested that if they could get someone else to play they might do better as he was shattered. The reply was to the effect that if they could have got anyone else they would have! How could he refuse such an invitation? He duly faced the Barbarians who were dispatched 14-3 and the following season became Newport's premier full-back. His success was such that within a dozen or so appearances he was selected to play for Wales against the English. His international debut was to be delayed, however, as whilst training at Glamorgan Wanderers' ground he went to retrieve a ball from a hedge and got the worst of an argument with a tree stump which punctured his knee causing him to miss the English and Scottish games.

He finally made his international debut on March 12th, 1955 at Cardiff, landing three conversions and a penalty as the Irish were defeated 21-9 and followed this by kicking ten points in Paris as Wales forestalled a French Grand Slam with a 16-11 victory which enabled Wales to share the championship. Owen's performance made him a hot favourite for the 1955 Lions tour of South Africa but he had to inform the

selectors that his college would not allow him to take the time off. The
following season saw him play in all four of Wales' matches and his
conversion of Derek Williams' try in a 5-3 victory over France allowed
Wales to take the Championship. It was to be his sixth and final appearance for Wales, games which had yielded him 26 points and a blossoming
reputation.

In October 1956 Owen became a professional with Halifax purely
through "newspaper talk". *"The Daily Herald"*, clearly short of hard
news, decided to indulge in a little speculation and carried the head-line
"Halifax offer Owen £5,000". It was the first Garfield had heard about it so
he telephoned the Halifax club, to whom it was also news. The thought
had anticipated the deed, however, and Halifax promptly offered him a
three year contract which he accepted. The story was so newsworthy that
the signing was televised live on "Sportsview" making Garfield the only
man to have signed away his amateur status with the nation as witness.
At the time of his capture there was talk about signing-fees being
rendered liable to tax so Owen's solicitor was instructed to frame a clause
making the Halifax club responsible for the payment of tax should the
law be altered. His task was to replace Tyssul Griffiths, by coincidence a
former Newport full-back himself who had played for Wales under both
codes (as a "Victory International" at Union) and had figured in many of
Halifax's trophy tilts and cup finals of the 1953-56 period. Griffiths was
a hard man to replace and was the current holder of the club goal-kicking
records at both Doncaster and Halifax. In a career spanning a decade
Griffiths had amassed 761 goals beginning at Hunslet and ending at
Dewsbury. Newport had also provided League with international full-
backs in D.R. Morgan (Swinton and Leeds) and Jack Evans (Hunslet) in
the post-war period, a rich harvest.

Halifax too had reaped a good crop of Welsh full-backs for apart
from Owen and Griffiths, Dick Davies of Swansea had given yeoman
service to the club in the twenties and thirties. Davies still holds the club
record for the number of consecutive appearances with 106 from his
debut in October 1925 to January 1928. Davies was noted for his match-
winning drop-goals but was very much the stay-at-home type of full-
back and did not score a try until his 198th game for the club almost five
years after his debut. His drop-goal at Wembley in the Cup Final of 1931
turned the tide of battle and inspired Halifax to defeat York. In the early
1950s another Swansea full-back in Gwylim Bowen held down the first
team spot before the arrival of Tuss Griffiths and it was to be another
Welshman in the shape of Ronnie James who would ultimately replace
Garfield Owen.

Owen's capture aroused great interest and 3,000 people turned up
to see him play his first game at Thrum Hall in a reserve fixture against
Bradford Northern "A" on October 27th, 1956. Garfield obliged by
kicking eight goals in a 37-7 victory. Just over five years later Owen was

to play in the same fixture on the same ground in his last appearance for the club, this time kicking twelve goals – a fitting rebuke to those who felt the club no longer needed him.

He could hardly have expected to make his first team debut where he did for it is not a usual occurrence for Rugby League clubs to play cross-Channel fixtures and Owen's debut may well be unique for Albi was the scene. The date was November 1st, 1956 and Halifax were playing in a European Championship match which was won by 19-11 with Owen landing two goals. Three days later he kicked three in a 24-9 victory at Carcassonne. On November 10th he played his first league fixture at Salford and failed to score in a 6-5 win. It was to be the only game of the 31 he played that season in which he did not kick a goal. By the end of the season he had kicked 91 goals which included three which beat Australia 6-3 a month after his debut. His form had been good enough to win him reserve selection for the Great Britain World Cup squad to Australia in the summer of 1957.

Despite this encouraging start to his life as a League player, Owen was soon to discover that all was not a bed of roses. From November 1957 until the following March he was demoted to the reserves with never a sight of first team football. Six goals in a victory over Bramley at the old Barley Mow on his return to the firsts indicated just how much his kicking had been missed and after landing eight in a 25-8 win at Featherstone he was chosen to represent a Rugby League XIII against France at Headingley on April 16th. The Rugby League XIII was essentially an Other Nationalities side and contained such great backs as Vollenhoven, Bevan, McLellan, Gabbitas, Stevenson and Lewis Jones. After missing a few shots at goal Jones handed over the kicking duties to Garfield who potted five as the French succumbed 19-8.

Garfield's wife, Marlene, who did not usually go to games was justifiably proud of her husband's performance but her delight changed to outraged wrath when the radio reports of the match credited Lewis Jones with her dearest's goals. Garfield recalls never having seen her so angry!

In 1957-58 Owen was joined at Thrum Hall by another big-name signing from Welsh Rugby Union when the club secured the services of the Neath forward Brian Sparks, holder of seven Welsh caps. Sparks, a dashing back-row forward, captained Halifax in 1960-61 and later moved to Salford. Like Owen, Sparks was a native of Llanharan, a village which also produced Dan Pascoe, a Bridgend International who turned professional with Leeds in 1927 and made a Wembley appearance with York in 1931. Another son of Llanharan who made good at League was Eynon Hawkins who won six Welsh RL caps (1949-53) whilst playing for Salford and Rochdale Hornets. League has much for which to thank Llanharan.

Owen was unfortunate in joining Halifax at a time when their great

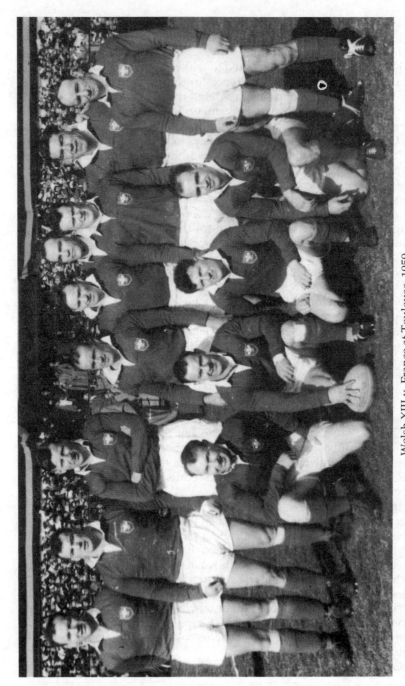

Welsh XIII v. France at Toulouse, 1959.
Back: John Thorley, Don Vines, Malcolm Davies, Rees Thomas, John Cheshire, Charlie Winslade, Gordon Lewis, George Parsons, Dai Moses
Front: Garfield Owen, Tommy Harris, Lionel Emmett, Graham Jones.

side of the fifties was breaking up and the club won nothing more than the Yorkshire League Championship (1957-58) during his time with them. He was doubly unfortunate in that Wales played no internationals during his career and the only opportunity he was afforded to wear the scarlet of his country was for a Welsh XIII against France at Toulouse in 1959, when no caps were awarded. He kicked a solitary goal as France won 25-8.

Despite his paucity in terms of winning cups and caps there was no gainsaying his value to his team and the esteem he commanded among the fans for Owen was extraordinarily reliable. Apart from his goal-kicking Garfield was a masterful tackler. His style was straight out of the text-book, clean and decisive. Those who saw him bring down Billy Boston repeatedly in a Halifax-Wigan game in 1961 will never see a better display of tackling. Boston, playing centre, was possibly the best tackle-breaker the game has known, but his frequent surges down the middle that day all foundered on Owen who took him at calf-level every time.

Another outstanding feature of Owen's play was his brilliance in gathering kicks. Hardly a match passed without him drawing the crowd's admiration for literally pulling his opponents' penalty kicks from over the touch-line. His positioning in this respect, as in all others, was immaculate and his arms were surely telescopic. Owen's field kicking was magnificent and probably all the more effective for being such an unusual feature of his play. Owen was in fact a kicking full-back at a time when the species was all but extinct. In the period when Owen flourished kicking in general play was almost anathema for it usually meant losing possession. To lose possession under the old unlimited tackle system was almost a capital offence yet Owen continued to kick for position and nobody complained. Owen was such a prodigiously long and accurate kicker that he very rarely failed to find his target and he was fortunate in that Halifax had hookers who could almost guarantee possession from the resulting scrummages. It was not too surprising that Owen was not discouraged from kicking when they could call upon Alvin Ackerley and Jobey Shaw, both test hookers, to clean up in the scrums.

There is little doubt that Garfield Owen was the last Rugby League player to resort to the "mark" as a means of extricating himself from trouble. The fair catch followed by a free kick had long been a disused facet of the game when Owen surprised and bewildered spectators and players by claiming marks as late as 1961. It is doubtful if any other player of his period could have got away with this tactic for the laws of the game decreed that the ball had to bounce into touch from a kick granted for a mark. A small detail like that did not deter Owen who recalls one occasion against Leigh when after claiming a mark near his line and close to the left touch-line nearly all the Leigh team lined that touch more or less challenging the "silly Welsh so-and-so" to bounce the ball into touch.

A Warrington defender halts Garfield Owen.
Johnny Freeman in support.

Owen scanned the field and noticed the Leigh left-winger on the far side at about half-way, knew he could kick it further than that and proceeded to find touch well behind the winger on the far side.

Although Owen liked running with the ball, he was not over-endowed with speed, so he stuck to what he did best and kicked the opposition to distraction. His experience in Union internationals had not exactly encouraged him to run the ball as "The Big Five" made it abundantly clear that full-backs who ran more than five yards could not expect to win any more caps.

When the Rugby League abolished the tap penalty in 1960 and made it obligatory to kick for touch Owen's value to his team soared even higher for there were few to rival him as a touch-kicker.

Owen succeeded Geoff Palmer to the Halifax captaincy in 1958-59 and kicked the first of five goal centuries in a season and the following season he broke Tuss Griffiths' club record of 149 goals in a season by landing 150. Four of these came in the final match of the campaign at Castleford and included a drop goal from half-way which Owen regarded as one of his finest kicks. Almost two decades later a Rugby League directive on scoring retrospectively took away his record as five goals had been kicked in a charity match and Tuss Griffiths again became the holder.

Owen's consistency as a goal-kicker was amazing. In 166 appearances for Halifax he failed to score only five times and in a career embracing almost 300 games only 17 saw his name missing from the goals sheet. His record in this respect is all the more meritorious as his career was played with only moderately successful sides. Opposing players, being human, sometimes erred and if they erred in their own half it usually meant two points to Owen's team. Whilst erring may be human, forgiving is divine, a past-time in which coaches do not overindulge. Coaches whose players erred when Owen was about were invariably not well-pleased as the full-back's goal-kicking often meant the difference between victory and defeat.

On a couple of occasions Garfield's kicking surprised even himself. In his second Union international against France at the Stade Colombes in 1955 he essayed a penalty kick from close on 50 yards. There was no appreciable wind and the kick was missing by about 15 yards when some benign spirit inexplicably altered its flight and sent it between the posts. Miracles apparently do happen. Another miracle occurred in a game at Fartown when Halifax scored at the open end as near to the corner flag as possible. Garfield knew there was no hope of converting the try as a gale force wind was howling at a right-angle straight down the pitch. Placing the ball, he turned to the crowd and invited them all to blow in the opposite direction. With Idwal Rees' words of wisdom telling him not to look up until he heard the cheering he let fly safe in the knowledge that he would not be hearing any cheering. Wrong again. Miraculously

Garfield Owen taking the great Brian Bevan into touch with the perfect tackle.

the oval never deviated until it had bisected the posts. Cheers!

The 1960-61 season was to be Owen's swan-song at Halifax and despite the club having only a mediocre campaign in the league Garfield had a splendid season, kicking his way into third place in the goal-scoring list, winning the inaugural club player-of-the-year award and being awarded the James Harrison Trophy, which is given annually by the Yorkshire Federation of Supporters Clubs to the fairest and most loyal player in the county, the judging being the prerogative of a panel of Lancastrian referees. Apart from testing their knowledge of the laws of the game by calling for marks, Owen never gave referees problems of a disciplinary nature. His demeanour on the field was exemplary and the furthest he ever fell from grace was to run the gauntlet of derision from the Threepenny Stand at the Boulevard. Playing against Hull he went to catch a high ball and most uncharacteristically made a complete hash of it. Angry with himself he proceeded to take it out on the ball which he hoofed 50 yards up the pitch whereupon he was instructed to go and fetch it. Anyone who has visited the Boulevard will not need reminding just how articulate the Threepenny stand can be!

At the start of the 1961-62 season Halifax had two first-class full-backs at their disposal for Ronnie James, a native of Ystalyfera, had been learning his trade in the "A" team for the past couple of years and was now vying for a first team spot. The upshot of the affair was that the club decided to part with Garfield and retain the younger man. Consequently Owen moved to Keighley where he was appointed captain-coach. Making his debut against Castleford on January 13th, 1962, he gave the Lawkholme Lane club more than four years service, continuing to give polished displays of the full-back's art and winning dozens of matches with his immaculate kicking. In his first full season with Keighley Owen took his side to promotion from the Second Division and shattered the club goal-kicking record of 106 held by the New Zealander, Joe Phillips, by landing 123 during the season. Seven goals kicked against Salford on May 22nd brought him the record. In the four years Owen spent with Keighley he set a new aggregate goals record for the club of 348 which surpassed Terry Hollindrake's figure of 320 goals but took Owen almost 100 games fewer. Owen's value to Keighley and a telling indication of his unremitting accuracy with the boot were never more graphically illustrated than in his last season (1964-65). During that campaign Owen appeared in all 37 of Keighley's league and cup fixtures and piled up 103 goals, an astonishing total when one considers the fact that his colleagues could only muster 47 tries between them. It is very much to be doubted whether anyone in the game's history has kicked such a mammoth ratio of goals to tries during the course of a complete season.

Owen bowed out of the game in a match against Dewsbury at Lawkholme on April 21st, 1965 to concentrate on his career. There is no doubt he could have carried on displaying his own brand of full-back

virtuosity for a few more seasons. Indeed Roy Francis wanted him at
Leeds to help bring out the best in his precocious charges who would
soon take the league world by storm. Francis must have had absolute
confidence in Garfield's magical boot for he promised him that all he
would have to do was to kick – his blossoming super-heroes would do
all the running. In the event Owen stuck to his decision to retire and
Francis recruited Bev Risman, gifted son of another Welsh maestro.

GARFIELD OWEN'S PLAYING RECORD FOR HALIFAX

	GAMES	TRIES	GOALS	POINTS
1956-57	31	—	91	182
1957-58	20	—	62	124
1958-59	28	1	102	207
1959-60	44	2	145	296
1960-61	41	1	130	263
1961-62	2	—	5	10
TOTALS	166	4	535	1,082

FOR KEIGHLEY

	GAMES	TRIES	GOALS	POINTS
1961-62	18	—	44	88
1962-63	35	2	123	252
1963-64	37	1	78	159
1964-65	37	—	103	206
TOTALS	127	3	348	705

All first-class matches:

	GAMES	TRIES	GOALS	POINTS
	296	7	890	1,801

Chapter 6

In the Shadow of Sullivan

It is the inescapable misfortune of all Rugby League full-backs to be compared to Jim Sullivan. Welsh full-backs are doubly unfortunate. At least English full-backs can aspire to be termed "greatest of English full-backs", for that title is likely always to remain open to question. The question as to who was the greatest of all Welsh full-backs no longer arises for Sullivan is universally regarded as the apotheosis of the position.

Nonetheless there have been many distinguished Welsh full-backs who have gone north to nobly serve an alien game. Perhaps the finest of the first wave of his breed to make a mark in the north was Richard Llewellyn Thomas who abandoned Newport for Oldham in 1897. Squat but solid, Dick Thomas gave Oldham long and honourable service. He was the Oldham full-back in the Cup Final of 1899 when the trophy first fell to a Lancashire club and in 1907 helped his club to win the Lancashire Cup for the first time. In the previous season (1906-07) he had captained Oldham in the finals of both the Challenge Cup and the Championship but had twice finished on the losing side. In that respect, at least, he was not so ill-starred as the Salford full-back, Dai Smith, a contemporary who had the misfortune to figure in three losing Challenge Cup Finals within four seasons (1900-1903). Smith was in fact the first Welsh Northern Union international full-back, appearing for the Other Nationalities against England at Wigan in 1904 in the sport's first international match, which was played 12-a-side.

The splendidly named Gomer Gunn was the next Welsh full-back to gain international honours. Gunn, a native of Treherbert, was selected for the Other Nationalities in 1905 and 1906 in 15-a-side matches and in 1907 in a 13-a-side international. The latter, the first with teams of thirteen, was, however, cancelled and several players were thus robbed of caps. Gunn joined Bradford in 1903-04 and was in their Challenge Cup-winning team of 1906. By 1908 he had so impressed Wigan that they parted with £200 to secure his transfer.

"Chick" (T.E.) Jenkins was the first full-back to wear a Welsh jersey in an international match when he was a member of the team that defeated New Zealand at Aberdare in 1908. A native of Cwm, Jenkins had been on the Hull register but returned to Wales to play for Ebbw Vale from where he won selection for the Australasian tour of 1910. To this day he remains the only player to be so honoured from a Welsh club. Although Jenkins won six of his seven Welsh caps as a full-back he toured as a centre. Leeds' Frank *"Bucket"* Young, formerly of Cardiff, did,

Chick Jenkins

Frank Young

however, make that tour as a full-back.

When Jim Sullivan came into the professional game in 1921 he was treading in the foot-steps of another great Welsh full-back at Wigan, a man revered as possibly the best full-back the game had seen until then. Gwyn Thomas' stature in the Rugby League pantheon should be immense but the accident of history which threw the omnipotent Sullivan into the League arena at the end of Thomas' career inadvertently served to diminish his greatness in the eyes of the Rugby League public who were blinded by Jim's all-consuming charisma for almost a quarter of a century.

Like Gunn, Gwyn Thomas was a native of Treherbert, where he first saw the light of day in 1893. A rugby prodigy, he appeared for Wales as a schoolboy international at the age of twelve, played first-class rugby at fourteen and was a Glamorgan cap by the time he was sixteen. As a Union player Thomas assisted Pontypridd, Neath, Cardiff and London Welsh and played representative rugby for Glamorgan, Middlesex and London, as well as winning a Welsh trial. On May 2nd, 1913, however, he forsook the amateur game and joined Wigan. An intelligent, perceptive and versatile player he often turned out at centre for Wigan, appearing in that role in the Lancashire Cup Finals of 1913 and 1914 but it was as a full-back that he won selection for the Australasian tours of 1914 and 1920.

Thomas was not a prolific scorer and obtained only 104 points (16 tries, 28 goals) in a career stretching over 178 games, a career savagely truncated through war and illness. Of his play the Official Tour Brochure for 1914 opined:

> *"He may best be described as a full-back of the aggressive order who pays little attention to orthodox rules. Thomas realizes the glorious possibilities of the professional code and does not favour in the slightest degree the passive defensive game".*

On both tours the other full-back was Oldham's Alf Wood, the former Gloucester and England RU player. On the 1914 trip Wood gained preference through his goal-kicking prowess for the big matches and Thomas' only test was the second against Australia. On his second tour, however, Wood had to play second fiddle to Thomas who was the vice-captain and figured in five of the six tests. Thomas had the honour of captaining the side in the third Australian and first New Zealand tests.

Thomas had joined Huddersfield in September 1919, the transfer costing £360. Whilst a Fartowner he played in all three tests against the 1921-22 Kangaroos making the last of nine test appearances in a 6-0 Ashes-winning victory at Salford. Although Huddersfield continued to enjoy outstanding success in the early post-Great War years Gwyn Thomas was unlucky in his quest for domestic honours as illness and injuries saw him miss all Huddersfield's finals except the Championship

Rugby League Championship Semi-Final 1923.

Gwyn Thomas kicks when challenged by Jack Evans of Swinton. Ex-Welsh R.U. winger, Frank Evans is wondering how Thomas got past him!

Tommy Rees – The only full-back to oust Jim Sullivan
from the Test Team.

Final of 1923 when the Fartowners went down to Hull Kingston Rovers. Huddersfield regarded Thomas so highly that he was appointed club captain over the immortal Wagstaff for the 1921-22 season, although the test selectors reversed their roles.

Thomas' appearances for Wales were restricted to games against England in 1913-14 and 1920-21. He captained his country in the latter match and also led the Other Nationalities that season against England when Wagstaff skippered the English. Oddly enough, it was Thomas' withdrawal as captain and full-back from the Welsh team to play Australia at Pontypridd in December 1921 that catapulted the young Sullivan into the international spot-light. His career ended in 1923 and he emigrated to the United States where he became the top executive at Pepsi-Cola. Over half a century after leaving Fartown Thomas repaid Huddersfield their £360 transfer fee as he felt he had not given the club adequate return for their outlay! Gwyn Thomas died in January 1984 at his home in Vero Beach, Florida, a far cry and a different world from South Wales and the north of England.

Once Sullivan had secured his place in the Welsh and test teams no other full-back of the inter-war period could seriously expect to oust him. Even so there were several very fine alternatives to the great man. All they could do, however, was wait and hope. The only Welsh full-backs whose hopes did not have to wait for ever were T.E. Rees of Oldham and Tommy Scourfield of Huddersfield, both ex-Union caps. Tommy "Guardsman" Rees, formerly of London Welsh, kicked 719 goals in his league career with Oldham and Broughton Rangers which covered 17 seasons. Success came early to Rees who gained preference over Sullivan for the first test against the 1929 Kangaroos in only his second season. Unfortunately for Rees Britain were walloped and Sullivan was never dropped again.

Tommy Scourfield, a native of Pontypridd who had played his senior rugby with Torquay and Devon, was even luckier. Sullivan was never dropped by Wales but in 1935 injury caused him to miss the international with England at Liverpool and Scourfield stepped up for his only cap. Men of the calibre of Dick Davies (Halifax), George Lewis (St. Helens) – capped three times for Wales at centre –, E.J. Owen (York), Fred Samuel (Hull, another Union cap) and Llew Williams (Salford) never got a look-in.

The post-war years, without Sullivan around, saw some excellent Welsh full-backs winning their fair share of international honours. Joe Jones, Jack Evans and Terry Price won test caps but perhaps the most successful of Welsh test full-backs of the post-war period was Glyn Moses. Moses, from Maesteg, joined Salford in 1948 where he played most of his early football in the three-quarters before settling at full-back in the 1950-51 season. At this point he was almost lost to the game and returned to Wales where he played a few games for the Cardiff RL club

Jack Evans (Hunslet), a fine full-back and winner of 4 Great Britain caps 1951-52.

in 1951-52. Fortunately, St. Helens has seen his potential and secured his transfer from Salford for £800 in 1952 after which he never looked back.

Moses was a running full-back of the highest class and a ferociously hard tackling machine. One thing at which he did not excel was the art of kicking and that deficiency probably cost him several test caps. He did, however, play nine tests for Great Britain between 1955 and 1957. He toured Australia twice – in 1957 as a member of the World Cup squad and in 1958 – and represented Wales in 1953 and the Other Nationalities in 1955. His strong running brought him more than fifty tries, a remarkable total for a full-back from his era and he won all the domestic honours open to him, including a Challenge Cup-winners' medal when Saints beat Halifax at Wembley in 1956. Glyn's brother, Dai, a forward, gave marvellous service to Salford for 13 years (1945-58) before crossing to Swinton. The two may hold a unique distinction for they were both sent off on October 28th, 1950 whilst playing for Salford in a local derby with Belle Vue Rangers. The disciplinary committee had no favourites, however, and both received two-match suspensions.

If Garfield Owen was the purist's ideal of the old-fashioned type of full-back his successor at Halifax was the very antithesis. Ronnie James, like Moses an ex-Maesteg player, was very much in the Moses mould, a full-back who loved to run and never passed up an opportunity to do so. James, a chunky, well-built player who joined Halifax in 1959 as a 21-year-old, was also a fine touch kicker and his goal-kicking prowess was considerable as his tally of over a thousand testifies. In fact only five Welshmen have kicked more goals than James in the history of the game. James gave many classic displays of goal-kicking during his career and landed plenty of drop-goals in an era when dropping goals was not the done thing. Even so he was often accused of being erratic in his goal-kicking being quite capable of missing from under the posts whilst equally capable of potting shots from the most difficult positions. Infuriating as he may have been on his bad days, his good days far outnumbered them.

Even though he was such a prolific kicker of goals it is as much for his entertainment value that fans remember Ronnie James, for when he had the ball in his hands there was never a dull moment. Head down, tree-trunk legs surging over the ground James would plough into, through or over the opposition like some sort of sawn-off Desperate Dan, absolutely refusing to be tackled. When he was eventually brought to ground the fun had not ended for he was like a veritable jack-in-the-box who could not wait to play the ball. Bodies would fly all over the place and Ronnie would usually get a penalty from the referee for being held down. Ronnie and the fans would then smile.

James, born at Ystalyfera on February 5th, 1938, never had the opportunity to play for Wales at League and won his only representative honour in 1965 when he played for a Commonwealth XIII against New

Ronnie James

Zealand at Crystal Palace. He did however win his share of medals as Halifax won the Championship, Yorkshire Cup and Eastern Division in the 1963-65 period.

RONNIE JAMES' PLAYING RECORD FOR HALIFAX

	GAMES	TRIES	GOALS	POINTS
1960-61	1	—	1	2
1961-62	35	4	74	160
1962-63	44	5	123	261
1963-64	38	8	105	234
1964-65	40	6	125	268
1965-66	31	2	90	186
1966-67	26	7	85	191
1967-68	36	3	85	179
1968-69	35	1	113	229
1969-70	36	4	81	174
1970-71	34	4	96	204
1971-72	15+1sub	1	50	103
TOTALS	371+1sub	45	1,028	2,191

All first-class matches:

	372+1 sub	45	1,030	2,195

Chapter 7

Lewis Jones
(Llanelli RU, Leeds RL, Wentworthville RL)

In a television interview in 1983 Lewis Jones, a teacher of mathematics in a girls' school in Leeds, described himself as *"a bit of a Compo in a room full of Norah Battys"*. A less flattering comparison to both the parties involved could scarcely be imagined. In one respect perhaps a parallel between Compo and Lewis Jones can be drawn. Compo's approach to the vicissitudes of life could only be described as casual and this was a term applied to Jones' attitude to rugby by his detractors. Great men in any sphere have their critics and Lewis Jones had his fair share. Most of those who were privileged to see him weave his magic, however, probably regarded him as something akin to the "last of the summer wine". Cliff Morgan, a kindred spirit to Jones, said on that same television programme:

> *I recall one Welshman claiming that he had been cured of shingles by touching Phil Bennett's boots. Another man announced on his deathbed, "I don't mind going to meet my creator now that I've seen Lewis Jones play Rugby"*

When Jones turned professional in 1952 the Rugby Union columnist Pat Marshall wrote:

> *"His genius lies in the unorthodox – doing the wrong thing superbly well and getting away with it. That and an ability to kick goals from almost any distance and angle"*.

Eleven years later, on the occasion of Jones' benefit with Leeds, Alfred Drewry of the *"Yorkshire Post"* wrote:

> *"My own assessment of Jones starts with the simple statement that he is the most talented Rugby player I have ever seen. In his mastery of the ball (in flight, in his hands or at his feet); in his sense of anticipation; in his ability to read a game and bring out the best of the players alongside him he is in a class by himself. But besides giving me more pleasure than any other player I have ever watched he has also caused me more exasperation than any other. Too often in his early days one got the impression that this moody genius was not using his talents to the full. But then, if he had been one of your all-out 80-minute players in every game . . . . . he would have burnt out years ago"*.

In *"Men in Black"*, written in 1978 to celebrate 75 years of New Zealand International Rugby, R.H. Chester and N.A.C. McMillan stated,

Lewis Jones

"In our opinion, no better full-back has toured New Zealand with a Rugby Union team since the war". This is praise indeed based upon the fact that Jones only played seven games in New Zealand on the 1950 Lions tour and especially when it is remembered that Jones thoroughly disliked playing in that position. Remember too that such fine full-backs as the South African S.S. Viviers, Frenchmen Claude Lacaze and Pierre Villepreux, and Lions of the calibre of Ken Scotland, Terry Davies, J.P.R. Williams and Andy Irvine have toured the Land of the Long White Cloud and it becomes clear just how good a performer Jones proved himself in those paltry seven games.

In 1969, whilst Jones was still parading his skills with Wentworthville in Australia at the age of thirty-eight, Eddie Waring wrote:

> *"Lewis Jones became Rugby League's most controversial figure, dividing the crowds into those who regarded him as a genius and those who claimed that he flattered to deceive. They were either 'Lewis Jones crazy' or scoffers because of the occasions when he appeared to be unwilling to shoulder his share of defensive work . . . . throughout his twelve tempestuous seasons on the Rugby League scene in Britain this fabulous entertainer and fantastic matchwinner became the greatest crowd-puller of them all".*

Whenever Lewis Jones is discussed or written about that word "genius" continually crops up. There is no doubt that in Jones' case the word is appropriate for as an attacking player he had all the gifts. Blistering speed off the mark, an unerring eye for an opening, a keen sense of anticipation, mesmeric hands that would almost make Paul Daniels seem ham-fisted, nimble footwork and mastery of every facet of kicking. Jones had all these but most importantly of all he had an ability to change pace which could only have been God-given and which baffled even the deadliest of tacklers. Jones' creative abilities can rarely have been matched and he had the nerve and confidence to indulge them. The coaching revolution would certainly have to make a detour around the Jones boy. Attack, attack, attack – that was all Jones appeared to think of, his critics said. Why not? – would be his fans' reaction. Jones himself repeatedly admitted that his rugby philosophy was based on all-out attack. At least everyone agreed! To those who complained, probably out of envy, that his tackling was not up to much the response must be that it did not matter. Worrying about Jones' defensive prowess was rather like fretting that Michelangelo might not be any good at cleaning windows. People did not pay to watch Lewis Jones tackle – let the others do that. There was adventure in the Welshman's soul – too much of the hard stuff might have dulled his sharpness. Besides Jones did eventually become a competent tackler but his critics had to have something to which to cling.

In 1958 Jones wrote in his aptly titled autobiography, *"King of Rugger"*:

"Ever since I started playing rugby seriously at the Gowerton County School during the war years I have never deviated from the belief that the game is first and foremost an attacking game. It is a belief that I put into practice from the very first moment of any match – club or international".

Jones was a great believer in applying the element of surprise in almost any situation. If sanity said keep the ball tight there would be Jones running the ball off his own line. He would kick when the text-book preached hold or pass and vice-versa. He would pass when a pass was not "on". For Jones the improbable was always at least possible and occasionally he would render the seemingly impossible probable. Like many of the truly great players he was willing to chance his arm, to take the risky option. Instinctively he would make the right choice and if there were rumblings amongst his critics over the unsoiled nature of his shirt when leaving the field, so be it. Jones would probably have sold his mother rather than be needlessly tackled.

Lewis Jones' career in Union was meteoric. He was born in Gorseinon on April 11th, 1931 and attended the same school as such notables as Haydn Tanner, Willie Davies, Onllwyn Brace and W. Rowe Harding, all of whom won caps for Wales as backs. As a schoolboy Jones had a preference for soccer but won Welsh caps for cricket and rugby, the latter as full-back against the French schoolboys in 1947-48 when his captain and fly-half was Carwyn James. It was soon apparent that Lewis was a star in the making and after a short period playing for his local club Gorseinon he graduated to first-class rugby with Neath. On call-up for the Royal Navy he found himself playing for Devonport Services from where he won his first full Welsh caps and his Union career ended with Llanelli. That coveted first Welsh cap came to Jones when he was only eighteen. He was selected to play against England on January 21st, 1950 and from the full-back position he set Twickenham alight with a daring display of running, creating a try out of nothing and kicking a penalty and a conversion in an 11-5 victory. The young hero was chaired from the field after this second Welsh victory at Twickenham in 40 years and Wales went on to win her first Grand Slam since 1911. Jones played in all four internationals – two at full-back and two at centre. The following season Jones felt the fury of the selectors as he was scape-goated after the famous Murrayfield massacre when Scotland beat the Welsh 19-0 – a national disaster. Among the Scottish victors that day was winger David Rose who was later to become a colleague of Jones at Headingley. Even the selectors realised that they were cutting off their noses to spite their faces and he was back in the national side in 1951 for the game against South Africa, this time on the left-wing. By the age of 20 in seven internationals he had figured in three positions. Although the Springboks won 6-3 it was a good season for the Welsh who again took the Grand Slam with Lewis Jones missing only the Scottish game through injury. The last of his ten appearances for Wales was in the 9-5 victory over France at Swansea on March 22nd, 1952, the game which sealed the Grand Slam. In those ten internationals Jones scored 36 points from six penalties and nine conversions.

Perhaps Jones' greatest impact as a Union player, however, was delivered when at the age of nineteen in 1950 he was called out to New Zealand for the Lions' tour as replacement for the Irish full-back, George Norton, who suffered a broken arm against Southland. The tour was already half-way through when Jones arrived but he had time to score 63 points in seven games in New Zealand and 92 points overall – only six points fewer than the tour's leading scorer, his Devonport colleague, Malcolm Thomas. Jones displaced Cardiff's Billy Cleaver for the fourth and final test and created one of the finest tries ever seen on the Eden Park ground in Auckland. 11-3 down, the Lions won a scrum on their own line and Rex Willis passed to his fly-half, the mercurial Jack Kyle. The pass never reached Kyle for Lewis burst between the halves as the extra man. The obvious thing to do was to kick but this was Lewis Jones. Befuddling the All Blacks with side-step and dummy he was off like a bolt from the blue. Around half-way was the formidable obstacle of full-back Bob Scott and chasing hard was the New Zealand Empire Games sprinter Peter Henderson, later to face Jones again as a winger with Huddersfield. Jones took Scott's tackle and lobbed a pass over Henderson into the eager arms of the Lions' own Olympic sprinter, Ken Jones who careered fifty yards to the posts for a sensational touchdown. Lewis Jones added the conversion to a penalty he had kicked earlier but the Lions were defeated 11-8.

The Lions moved on to Australia where Lewis played in both tests which were won 19-6 and 24-3. In the first at Brisbane Jones set up a record in international games by scoring sixteen points from a try, a drop-goal, two penalties and two conversions.

Not surprisingly Jones soon earned himself the title "Golden Boy" of Welsh Rugby Union and Welsh fans were aghast when it was learnt that he had signed for Leeds in November 1952. One newspaper reported that the *"Llanelli secretary, Mr. Sid Williams, had nothing to say, but decided to go to the pictures 'to drown my misery'."* Perhaps his misery was so intense that he could no longer distinguish between the cinema and the public house!

The cost of obtaining Lewis Jones' signature was astronomical for Leeds, the fee being reported as £6,000 – £1,000 more than any club had ever paid for a player from either the Union or League ranks. In the event the signing proved cheap at the price. His debut took place two days after his signing on November 8th, 1952 when he appeared as full-back against Keighley at Headingley. A crowd of 17,000 came to pass judgement as Jones bagged seven goals but missed a lot more in a 56-7 stroll. He had made a satisfactory start to his professional career but was soon to find that his new game was not a bed of roses. His third game was against the

A cartoonist's view of Lewis Jones in 1961.

touring Australians and Leeds were annihilated 45-4 and one newspaper reported, *"McLellan looked much more like a £6,000 man than Lewis Jones. The Welshman spent the second half limping on the wing with a sore ankle, but even before that he had never been in the game except for his two goals and a first minute dash which ended in touch near the corner"*.

Worse was to follow. In only his eighth appearance for his new club at Batley on January 24th, 1953 Jones went down to a fair tackle by John Etty and fractured his arm and his first season was ended after only a couple of months. The critics no doubt felt vindicated when Jones failed to strike form on his return after injury at the start of 1953-54 and the Golden Boy was relegated to the reserves. By October, however, he was back in the first team causing havoc to the opposition and from then on things began to go right. In the first three weeks of November Leeds beat Hull K.R. 56-5, Wakefield Trinity 46-5 and Castleford 48-14 and Jones' contributions were ten goals and a try, eight goals and nine goals and a try respectively – 60 points in the three games. By the end of the season, in all games, he had amassed 302 points from 124 goals and 18 tries and his record-shattering career was well and truly launched. By December he had had his first taste of international Rugby League kicking five goals for Wales against France at Marseilles. In a splendid match the Welsh went down 23-22 and the Rugby League, in its infinite wisdom, abandoned the practice of maintaining Wales as an international side until it was resurrected in 1968. Jones therefore was never to play for Wales again.

1954 was scheduled for the tenth Great Britain tour of Australasia and Jones was firmly in the running for one of the centre positions. He was duly selected to play in the first tour trial at Headingley. His opposing centre, Duggie Greenall of St. Helens, one of the most ferocious of tacklers, had shattered quite a few reputations previously and was seen as an acid test of Jones' ability and temperament. Jones passed the test with honours and was selected as one of the tour centres along with Greenall, Phil Jackson (Barrow) and Ernie Ashcroft (Wigan). Also selected among the party was Lewis' club colleague Drew Turnbull, a speedy Scottish winger who had run in 41 tries during the season. The captain was to be Welsh stand-off Dickie Williams who had left Leeds for Hunslet earlier in the season. Billy Boston, even newer to League than Jones, Ray Price and Tommy Harris were other Welshmen in the party.

Although the Ashes were lost 2-1 to the Aussies, the tour was a major triumph for Jones who broke records all along the way. Injuries to fullbacks Jack Cunliffe and Ted Cahill meant that Jones played in that position in 16 of his 21 games. In the course of the tour he kicked 127 goals and scored eight tries to total 278 points, a record which still stands. The old record for a British touring side had been 223 points (110 goals) gathered by that other great Welshman Jim Sullivan in 1932 in exactly as many matches. The previous record for any tour had been set by Puig

Aubert, the roly-poly, chain-smoking French full-back who had claimed 221 points on the 1951 tour. If Jones had often been referred to as casual Puig Aubert could only be described as laid-back in modern parlance.

Among his achievements was a 15 goal haul at Canberra against Southern District – the biggest bag of his professional career – 12 goals against Canterbury and 11 against Wellington.

Selected as a centre but pressed into service as the main full-back it should have come as no surprise, in Jones' case, that he made his test debut on the right wing! The occasion was the first test at the Sydney Cricket Ground on June 12th before a crowd of 65,884. Jones kicked three goals but unusually for him it was to be no fairy-tale introduction to the hardest form of rugby football as Australia ran roughshod over the British 37-12. It was the Australian right winger, Noel Pidding, who stole the show scoring a test record 19 points (8 goals and a try).

The tourists pulled themselves together and went through their next seven fixtures in Queensland like a dose of salts scoring 255 points in the process. The second test was played on July 3rd at the 'Gabba in Brisbane where Jones had set up his Rugby Union test record four years previously. This time Jones was at full-back and it was Britain's turn to demolish the opposition to the tune of 38-21. Pidding saw his record eclipsed as Jones peppered the posts to land ten goals, two of which were dropped. No British player has ever exceeded Jones' ten goals in a test although it has been equalled and only Roger Millward has equalled the 20 points for Britain in tests against Australia.

The third test at Sydney was a much tighter affair with Pidding's four goals to Jones' two making the difference as Australia won 20-16. Remarkably the series saw both land 15 goals. Jones played full-back in all three tests in New Zealand landing a further ten goals as Britain won the series 2-1.

The tour had confirmed all that Jones' devotees had ever thought about him. Within a very short space of time he had become acknowledged as something "completely different" and he was big box-office. On returning from the tour, however, he was one of the many tourists who declined the chance to represent Britain in the inaugural World Cup competition in France in October and November 1954 when Dave Valentine's squad confounded all the critics in lifting the trophy. He did however accept his invitation to play in the next World Cup held in Australia in 1957 when he was again selected as a centre but found himself playing stand-off against France and Australia as Ray Price had been injured. Britain had been favourites to retain the cup but after easily defeating the French they fell ignominiously to Australia (6-31) and then to New Zealand (21-29). Jones certainly was not to blame but he never played test rugby again and it became clear that for someone in high places he was *persona non grata*. His test career spanned only three years during which he made fifteen appearances in the red, white and blue ranks, scoring in every single match and totalling 147 points (66 goals, 5 tries). He played six of those tests at full-back, six at left-centre, two at stand-off and one on the wing to underline just how versatile a performer he was. In the three match series against France in 1957 he kicked 21 goals and in each game scored a try to claim 51 points. His try in the second test at Toulouse came from 75 yards and enabled the British to draw the game 19-19 after they had trailed 17-2.

It was fortunate indeed for the British selectors that Jones was contemporary with some wonderful centres (Eric Ashton, Alan Davies, Neil Fox and Phil Jackson, to name a few) and so his omission was perhaps not so greatly felt as it would have been in leaner times. He was fortunate enough, however, to appear in possibly the greatest of three-quarter lines when, on the disbandment of the Wales XIII, he figured at centre in the final two internationals played by the much lamented Other Nationalities in 1955-56. The Others beat England 33-16 and France 32-19 to lift the International Championship. Jones' winger was bouncing Billy Boston of Wigan who scored five tries with a little help (not that Billy ever needed much help) from Lewis who kicked ten goals and scored a try. The other three-quarters were Halifax's clever, thrustful ex-All Black centre Tommy Lynch whose partner was Australian Brian Bevan, arguably the world's finest winger of any era. Jones' final representative recognition came in 1963 when he captained a Welsh XIII against France at Toulouse. Jones played stand-off that day to his Leeds scrum-half colleague Colin Evans, winner of a solitary Union cap against England in 1960.

Even if the international selectors did not like him, the Leeds fans certainly did and his club career continued to be successful. He won all the domestic honours open to him as Leeds won the Yorkshire League Championship in 1954-55, 1956-57 and 1960-61, the Yorkshire Cup in 1958, the Challenge Cup in 1957 and the Championship in 1961. In the process Jones kept breaking records. The list reads:

Most goals in a match for Leeds	13	v. Blackpool 19th August, 1957
Most points in a match for Leeds	31	v. Bradford N. 22nd August, 1956
Most goals in a season for Leeds	166	in 1956-57
Most points in a season for Leeds	431	in 1956-57
Most goals in a career for Leeds	1,244	
Most points in a career for Leeds	2,920	
World record points in a season	496	in 1956-57 (including representative matches)
World record goals in a season (equalled)	194	in 1956-57 (including representative matches)

Of all the above records only the final one has not been surpassed. Unquestionably Jones' most enduring feat was his creation of the world record for points in a single season set in 1956-57. The old record, inevitably, had been the work of Jim Sullivan who had aggregated 406 points (194 goals, 6 tries) in 1933-34. Jones scored his points thus:

	A	T	G	P
For Leeds	43	33	166	431
Tests v. France	3	3	21	51
Rest of League v. G. Britain	1	—	4	8
Rugby League v. Australians	1	—	3	6
Totals	48	36	194	496

Sullivan's points record fell on March 30th at Odsal when Jones kicked two goals as Leeds beat Whitehaven 10-9 in the Challenge Cup semi-final whilst his third goal in a 12-22 defeat at Oldham in the Championship Semi-final on May 4th brought him a share in the goal-kicking record. Of the 48 games he failed to score in only two – at St. Helens on April 6th, when Leeds were thrashed 44-3 and at Wembley on May 11th in the only Challenge Cup Final he played. Fortunately, in a very closely contested game, the tries scored by Quinn, Hodgkinson and Robinson were sufficient to thwart Barrow 9-7. Jones, the precocious young player, admitted developing nerves late in his career and claimed his knees felt like jelly all through his solitary Wembley appearance.

Most of Jones' early football with Leeds was as a centre but from 1959-60 on he began to figure more prominently at stand-off and it was from this pivotal position that he led his club to its first ever Championship in season 1960-61. Leeds, winners regularly of Rugby League's other trophies and always in the vanguard for enterprise and innovation, had quite amazingly never achieved the status of Champions, having been defeated finalists five times and lost eight times at the semi-final stage. It had seemed to the Headingley fans that the Championship was to be eternally denied to Leeds but, brilliantly captained by Jones, the club finished at the top of the table winning 30 of its 36 games and after disposing of St. Helens in the semi-final met Warrington at Odsal Stadium in the final. More than 52,000 people saw the Golden Boy give one of his most memorable performances, dictating the play, debilitating the opposition and sending the Leeds followers into ecstasy as he cut through to score the final try which sealed a 25-10 victory – he also contributed five goals.

Throughout his career Lewis Jones was fortunate to play alongside fine players who helped his genius to flourish. His early days at Head- ingley were spent with great players such as Bert Cook, Dickie Williams, Arthur Clues, Keith McLellan, Drew Turnbull, Ted Verrenkamp and Jeff Stevenson. The latter part of his time at Leeds saw Wilf Rosenberg, Ken

Lewis Jones

Thornett, Derek Hallas, Don Robinson, Brian Shaw and Geoff Wriglesworth aiding and abetting the Welsh maestro. Even amongst players as talented as these it was Jones that people really wanted to see. It did not matter which position he played for his skills would have shone through even if he had been selected as hooker. Arguments will always rage as to whether he was more suited to one position than another but the records show that in 385 games for Leeds he appeared 231 times as a centre, 117 as stand-off, 35 as full-back and once on each wing.

Even if he had not been such an irresistible attacking force Jones would have been revered in both rugby codes simply for his prowess as a kicker. His accuracy and power as punter, drop-kicker or place-kicker have seldom been matched. Rugby Union adherents still recall the day in 1950 at Twickenham when Jones played for the Navy against the Army. Breaking in a pair of new boots Lewis christened them by kicking a penalty goal from five yards inside his own half and two yards from touch. The goal was computed to be at least a seventy yarder and generously cleared the bar. Everyone on the ground was astounded especially the Navy captain who had only asked for the attempt to be made to allow his forwards a breather. His kicking feats as a League player were legion and included kicking ten or more goals on ten occasions. Jones kicked goals with his right foot in a somewhat stiff-legged action but with a perfect follow-through. He could kick goals from vast distances using a run-up of only two or three steps and believed that a longer run impaired his timing and consequently diminished his accuracy. In his later years he gave his critics more ammunition by placing the ball upright for even the longest of kicks, contrary to the text-books. It did not make any difference for he was just as deadly. When the ball was wet and heavy he employed the round-the-corner method so beloved of modern kickers as he maintained there was more to hit with the instep.

Whilst with Leeds Jones developed the famous "hanging pass" in conjunction with Colin Evans. As Jones received the ball he would simply dart away having lobbed the ball into mid-air where, as if suspended on a heavenly string, it would await collection by a fast-following support.

Jones played his final game for Leeds on Easter Monday, 1964 against Halifax at Headingley before taking his talents to the other side of the world to become player-coach of Wentworthville in the Sydney Second Division. In the half-dozen years he spent in Australia he scored close on a thousand points and led his club to five Second Division Premierships.

If the legendary Arthurian sorcerer Merlin has ever had a sporting reincarnation it was assuredly that magician of the oval ball, Benjamin Lewis Jones and fortunate were those who witnessed the spells he cast.

LEWIS JONES' PLAYING RECORD FOR LEEDS

	GAMES	TRIES	GOALS	POINTS
1952-53	8	3	20	49
1953-54	28	18	111	276
1954-55	31	13	104	247
1955-56	22	15	76	197
1956-57	43	33	166	431
1957-58	39	14	139	320
1958-59	39	16	126	300
1959-60	31	5	109	233
1960-61	39	10	105	240
1961-62	39	7	117	255
1962-63	39	7	105	231
1963-64	27	3	66	141
TOTALS	385	144	1,244	2,920

All first-class matches:

	429	158	1,449	3,372

N.B. The above figures exclude the 3 games Jones played for the British XIII against a French XIII in South Africa in 1957 in which he scored 29 goals, 5 tries, 73 points.

Chapter 8

David Watkins

(Newport RU, Salford RL, Swinton RL)

In the mid-1960s David Watkins was arguably the world's best Rugby Union fly-half and certainly the most entertaining in an era when international Union matches generated as much excitement as a tour round the local mortuary. As a stand-off in Rugby League he never really delivered the goods despite the record fee placed around his neck on turning professional in October, 1967. Even so Watkins became one of the most respected and successful of all Rugby Union converts to League who more than recompensed Salford for their £16,000 outlay. His value to the club as crowd-puller, entertainer, record-breaker and match-winner was incalculable.

Watkins, a native of Blaina, was born on March 3rd, 1942. His childhood and youth followed what appears to have been the classical pattern in moulding a Welsh rugby superstar. Son of a coalminer, the young Watkins' first love was soccer but inevitably it was rugby which he espoused. His career began at Glanyrafon Secondary Modern School as a scrum-half but he soon gravitated to his natural position at fly-half and progressed to the Cwmcelyn Youth side where he won honours with Monmouthshire Youth and ultimately with Wales Youth.

Naturally enough several of the senior Welsh clubs encouraged David to join them but it was to be at Rodney Parade in the famous black and amber hoops of Newport that he made his name. His debut took place on September 2nd, 1961 when he ran in a 40 yards try in a 34-6 victory over Penarth and from then on his grip on the fly-half spot was never seriously in jeopardy. His first three seasons were spent under the captaincy of Welsh international forwards Bryn Meredith, Glyn Davidge and Brian Price but by 1964, aged 22, the captaincy had fallen to Watkins and he was to retain it until he went north. His career as a Newport player encompassed 202 matches during which he totalled 288 points, including 32 tries and 55 drop-goals. Strangely enough two of his scrum-half partners preceded him into the professional ranks where they both won Welsh caps. Bob Prosser, whom David was later to partner at Salford, joined St. Helens whilst his successor Cliff Williams, a former captain of Cross Keys, threw in his lot with Hunslet and latterly Batley.

Undoubtedly the greatest match in which David Watkins played for Newport was that of October 30th, 1963 when Wilson Whineray's All Blacks met with defeat for the only time on their tour of Britain. It was not a day for running at rain-swept Rodney Parade and Watkins kicked judiciously to keep the New Zealand full-back Don Clarke continuously

David Watkins
(Courtesy "The Rugby Leaguer")

on the hop whilst the Newport forwards held everything the tourists threw at them. The only score came after a typical Watkins break which helped to set up the position from which John Uzzell's drop-goal sent all Wales into ecstasy.

Watkins made his debut for Wales against England on January 19th, 1963 opposite the elegant Richard Sharp of the Wasps. Five other Welshmen appeared for the first time in scarlet jerseys adorned with the Prince of Wales' feathers including David's scrum-half Clive Rowlands, the captain. It was not an auspicious occasion for England won 13-6, a feat they have not performed at Cardiff subsequently. Watkins retained his place in all four internationals, dropping a goal against Ireland but finishing on the winning side only at Murrayfield when the Scots were beaten 6-0.

The laws of the game at the time and the influence and limitations of Rowlands at scrum-half meant that Watkins' first few matches for Wales were spent watching his captain incessantly kicking for touch. The furthest the stand-off had to run was invariably from the dressing-rooms to the pitch. Still the Welsh team improved to the extent that a share in the Championship with Scotland was obtained in 1964 when the Welsh were undefeated. David scored a sensational try – his first for Wales – in the 15-6 win over Ireland in Dublin. Wales won the Triple Crown and the Championship in 1965 and retained the Championship in 1966 with Watkins playing in all eight matches. Then after playing in 18 successive internationals he was left out of the Welsh team to play Australia in 1966, his place going to Barry John who also played in the first Championship match at Murrayfield. Wales lost both games and David was reinstated for the Irish game at Cardiff and awarded the captaincy for the first time. Wales lost 3-0 but he remained captain for the French match in Paris where his drop-goal proved to be his final score for Wales who went down 20-14. The match was notable for being the occasion of Gareth Edwards' debut and the last appearance of Terry Price who was soon to join Bradford Northern. The Welsh managed to salvage something from their last game of the season, however, when Watkins led them to a spectacular 34-21 victory over the English at Cardiff. The game will forever be remembered as "Jarrett's Match" as David's club-mate Keith Jarrett scored 19 points on his debut. Jarrett, of course, was another Welsh "golden boy" destined to go north.

The English match was to be Watkins' last match for Wales. He had won 21 Welsh caps – at the time more than any other Welshman to turn professional – and had played six tests for the British Isles in Australasia in 1966, captaining the Lions in the second and fourth tests in New Zealand.

His successor, Barry John passed the following comments on Watkins:

> *"I could not learn much from him, since our ways of playing the game were poles apart. But he was undeniably a fine stand-off half, in the explosive style of a Cliff Morgan or Phil Bennett. I thought of him as a 'counter-puncher' – that is, he waited for tacklers to commit themselves and then – pfft! – he was gone. He could be contained by a cautious stifling of his options, but one lapse of concentration by defenders usually proved fatal".*

> (from *"The Golden Years of Welsh Rugby"*)

Whilst comparisons may be odious they are nonetheless interesting. Watkins, like Cliff Jones and Cliff Morgan, played under conditions which militated against their free-running style. Barry John, Phil Bennett and their successors operated in an era when the game became more fluid and entertaining and consequently had greater opportunities to display their attacking wares. Watkins with his instant acceleration was sensational enough in his own era. How much more devastating would he have been playing in the Welsh teams of the Second Golden Era?

Halifax, Leeds and St. Helens had all tried to tempt the Welsh wizard north at various stages in Watkins' career but it was Salford, under the direction of go-ahead Chairman Brian Snape, who finally got his signature on a Rugby League registration form. The fee was reported to total £16,000 including £1,000 due at the start of each of his first five seasons. There were those who thought the little Welshman would not last anything like five seasons in the hurly-burly of Rugby League. David proved the sceptics hopelessly wrong for Salford had twelve seasons inestimable service from him.

Salford put Watkins straight into the first team in a game against Oldham at the Willows on October 20th, 1967. By a strange coincidence he was not the only son of Blaina and ex-Cwmcelyn Youth player on the pitch that night as Oldham's right-winger Mike Elliott was also in the early stages of a long and honourable career. The impact that Watkins' capture had on the Salford public can be gauged from the fact that three days earlier 2,500 had turned up to watch them beat Whitehaven but 12,000 were present to run the rule over the new man. They must have been well satisfied for the stand-off scored a superb seventy yard try, dropped two goals and won the man of the match award as his team triumphed 12-6. He also showed that he was an excellent handler, an efficient coverer and a magnificent touch-finder. Salford had struck gold.

In his second season at Weaste Salford made Watkins club captain but not even the most fervent optimist would have forecast that he would be leading out his team at Wembley before the season was over. Such was the case, however, for favoured with home draws Salford despatched Batley, Workington and Widnes before beating Warrington 15-8 at the semi-final stage. It was Salford's first appearance in the Challenge Cup Final for 30 years and Watkins was emulating the deeds of his great

Welsh predecessor Gus Risman. The Final was a bitter disappointment as Salford never approached their best form and a drab game ended in an 11-6 victory for Castleford. That 1969 Final was to be Watkins' only appearance at Wembley. His fellow country-man Ron Hill, formerly of Cardiff, scored all the Reds' points with three penalty goals.

Promising though Watkins' early days at the Willows were he was not really suited to the role of stand-off in his new game. His startling speed off the mark remained his great asset but he was perhaps, at twenty-five years old, too old a dog to alter his style and master the intricacies of Rugby League half-back play. Men such as Alan Hardisty, Mick Shoebottom, Harold Poynton, Roger Millward, Cliff Hill, Frank Myler and Phil Kitchin, to name but a few, were all born and bred in the game and were clearly all ahead of Watkins if it came to selection for representative rugby. Watkins' mazy running could delight and infuriate spectators. It could also lead him up blind alleys, as it were, and one got the impression that his manoeuvres were so instinctive and unexpected that his colleagues were often as confused as the opposition. David also became the focus of heavy marking and he was a ready target for the game's hatchet men. Fortunately, he was brave and tough enough to survive and for so small a player he was surprisingly aggressive and strong.

The 1970-71 season proved to be a turning point in David's career. Until that season David had not been the club's goal-kicker and indeed had no real reputation as a place-kicker for as a Union player he had only placed 12 goals for Newport. His artistry as a drop-goaler, however, had continued to flourish in League. Now he was entrusted with the goal-kicking duties and his success was staggering. Watkins did as much as anyone to popularize the round the corner style of kicking so prevalent today and for a player of his physical stature he had a tremendous range. By the close of the season he had shattered Risman's club records set in 1933-34 having booted 155 goals and collected 358 points. The following season he extended those records to 192 goals and 474 points (including 30 tries). Yet even those figures paled in comparison with his achievements of 1972-73 when he kicked a world record 221 goals for Salford eclipsing the previous record of 219 set by Oldham's Bernard Ganley in 1957-58. He had equalled Ganley's record in the final league match of the season in a 15-3 home victory over Wigan when he had scored two tries in addition to three goals. The record became his in the Premiership play-off first round when he landed two goals in a surprise home defeat by Rochdale Hornets. He had gone into that game against Hornets needing eight points to pass Lewis Jones' all-time record figure of 496 points in a season but the defeat cost Watkins the chance to claim a new record.

By the time Watkins finally called it a day at Salford he had dwarfed Risman's aggregate totals having kicked 1,241 goals and amassed 2,907 points. He had also equalled Risman's club record by kicking 13 goals in

Stuart Ferguson (ex-Swansea RU) who scored in all of Leigh's matches in 1970-71. Ferguson is the only Welshman other than David Watkins to perform this feat.

a 65-3 victory over Keighley on January 7th, 1972. In no fewer than 10 matches for Salford he landed ten or more goals including ten against the 1972 New Zealand World Cup Team. Among the more exotic of his scoring feats was a hat-trick of tries against Barrow scored in only 4 $^1/_2$ minutes and claimed to be the fastest on record, whilst on another occasion he scored all 14 of Salford's points (4 tries and a goal) at the Boulevard and yet finished on the losing side as Hull won 22-14 (5th March, 1972)! In seasons 1972-73, 1973-74 and 1975-76 Watkins was the league's leading goal-kicker and points-scorer, also topping the points list in 1971-72. Only six men have scored more points that the Blaina boy in the history of the game and he is unique in twice in consecutive seasons performing the feat of playing and scoring in every game in a season. He did this in 1972-73 and 1973-74. The feat has been accomplished 12 times in the history of the game with Leigh's Stuart Ferguson (ex-Swansea) being the only other Welshman to do it in 1970-71.

Watkins' durability is reflected in the fact that he played 140 consecutive games for Salford between April 1971 and April 1974, ten more than the previous club record by another Welshman, Bert (H.C.) Day, a hooker who won Welsh caps under both codes. Coincidentally Day had been signed from Newport. His consistency as a goal-kicker is mirrored in the fact that Watkins kicked goals in 92 consecutive matches between August 1972 and April 1974 – another record in British Rugby League.

Apart from marking the commencement of David Watkins' career as "Super-kick" 1970-71 saw him embark upon a new career at centre. By February, 1971 he had played over 120 games for Salford and all had been at stand-off but a new face was beginning to challenge for the number six shirt and his talent could not be denied its reward. The man was Ken Gill, a masterly purveyor of the ball and a player who could orchestrate attacking ploys to perfection. Gill would attain test status and became a key player at the Willows. It must have been with some misgivings that David found himself pushed back to centre for he certainly had not the physique normally associated with the position. His debut as a centre took place on February 12th, 1971 in a home win over Hull and Watkins was never to start a game at stand-off for Salford again. The move out to centre gave him that little bit more time to exploit his brilliant acceleration and he was still near enough the action to dominate with his boot when necessary. His rapport with fellow centre Chris Hesketh was amazing although the two were very different in style. Hesketh, known to his team as "the snake", was tall and wiry and a marvellous side-stepper and had come up through the ranks with Wigan. He and Watkins were to share a well-deserved testimonial in 1977-78 as well as touring Australasia together in 1974. So successful was Watkins' conversion to centre that in his first full season in the position he went over for thirty tries. Within weeks of his debut at centre he had won the first of his six test selections when he appeared in a 24-2 victory over France at St.

Helens.

In 1972 he led Salford to their first Cup success for many years when he scored 13 points in a 25-11 Lancashire Cup Final win over Swinton but 1973-74 was probably his most successful season at the Willows. Watkins played in all 45 of Salford's games, kicked 182 goals, scored 24 tries, helped his new wing-partner, the jet-propelled Keith Fielding to score 46 tries and led Salford to the Rugby League Championship for the first time since 1939. At the season's end he was rewarded with a place in the 1974 touring party to Australasia. Although Watkins was captain at Salford the British selectors appointed his colleague Chris Hesketh tour captain and it was Hesketh who succeeded Watkins as skipper the following season at the Willows.

The tour was not the success for which Watkins must have hoped as he suffered a severe knee injury which restricted his appearances to only eight, including the first test against Australia at Brisbane. On returning home the injury, coupled with problems caused by promotion at work, caused him to retire from the game. His retirement proved premature, however, for Salford persuaded him to restart when injuries to key members of the team hit the club hard. By January 1975 he was back in the centre helping Salford to lift the B.B.C. Floodlit Competition Trophy and by February he was playing for Wales in his former position at stand-off in partnership with Salford scrum-half Peter Banner. Even more re-markably, a year after his disastrous tour he was back again Down-under leading Wales in their bid for the World Championship.

Watkins played 16 times for Wales as a League player and was captain on 14 occasions. He scored two tries, four drop-goals and 32 placed-goals for his country and, combining League and Union, his international career spanned the period 1963-79. His League caps were won as stand-off (5), centre (5) and full-back (6).

After carving out a career at centre Watkins astounded everyone once more when in 1975 he was induced to replace full-back Paul Charlton, possibly the greatest of all attacking full-backs, who had returned to his native Cumbria. Predictably, however, David was a huge success for in that position he had more room than ever in which to launch his lightning attacks and although he was at a disadvantage when trying to stop big men near the line his speed allowed him to take attackers from the side or behind when further out. That first season at full-back (1975-76) saw Salford once again crowned Rugby League Champions. It seemed as if Watkins could go on forever and he was indeed far from finished for at the end of the following season he was chosen to go Down-under yet again – this time as coach to Great Britain's World Cup team which performed wonders before going down 13-12 in a desperately close final to Artie Beetson and his all-conquering Austra-lian team. Although David was no longer a contender for a test place he did play in the majority of the ordinary tour matches.

David Watkins in his Swinton days
(Courtesy "The Rugby Leaguer")

Time finally ran out for Watkins at Salford on April Fools' Day 1979 when after playing in an 8-5 victory at Rochdale he retired for the second time. But Rugby League was unwilling to give him up so easily and Salford's neighbours Swinton persuaded him to play the 1979-80 season with them in the Second Division. The Lions had the benefit of his expertise for 20 matches during which he added a further 53 points to his gargantuan tally.

Having finished his stint at Swinton the Rugby League world could have been forgiven for thinking that he had finished for good with the game but it was not to be for 1981 saw the birth of the Cardiff City Blue Dragons at Ninian Park. It was a little like preaching Methodism in the Vatican and for three years David was to play the role of John Wesley. The experiment failed but no-one ever questioned David Watkins' determination and efforts to make it succeed. He was even turning out for Cardiff in odd games during 1982-83 at the age of forty. There are those who believe he may yet make another comeback!

Chance would be a fine thing – ask them at Salford!

DAVID WATKINS' PLAYING RECORD FOR SALFORD

	GAMES	TRIES	GOALS	POINTS
1967-68	24	9	15	57
1968-69	34	9	14	55
1969-70	36	15	18	81
1970-71	41	16	155	358
1971-72	44	30	192	474
1972-73	47	17	221	493
1973-74	45	24	182	436
1974-75	15+1sub	3	11	31
1975-76	37+1sub	13	158(4dg)	351
1976-77	34	6	125(2dg)	266
1977-78	34	3	109(8dg)	219
1978-79	14	2	41(2dg)	86
TOTALS	405+2subs	147	1,241	2,907

All first-class matches:

	460+12subs	154	1,342(29dg)	3,117

dg indicates drop-goals valued at one point.

Chapter 9

Thrum Hall Flyers

Wingers of Welsh extraction have scored over a thousand tries for the Halifax club, an amazing statistic in view of the fact that some first-class Welsh Union clubs will not be able to say the same of their wingers. On the other hand, it is not such a surprising figure when one remembers that the Halifax club until recent times always seemed to have at least one Welshman on their flanks. For many years Welsh wingers were the rule rather than the exception on the windy heights of Thrum Hall and the club's recruitment of the breed dates back to the earliest years of the Northern Union.

Oddly enough, the first Welsh winger to be signed by Halifax never played for them but was employed as club secretary from 1901 to 1912. This was Cardiff's Arthur Ricketts who scored 34 tries in 55 appearances for that celebrated club in the years before the turn of the century and played alongside the glorious Gwyn Nicholls. Among his team-mates were "Hockey" Driscoll and Viv Huzzey who were to find fame and fortune with Hull and Oldham respectively.

It was probably Ricketts' knowledge of the Welsh scene and his contacts which brought several fine Welsh wings to his adopted club. "Wax" (W.W.) Williams, a former colleague at Cardiff and related by marriage to Nicholls, was Ricketts' first import. Williams had been top try-scorer for Cardiff with 19 to his credit in 1900-01 but decided to take the rewards the Northern Union could offer and joined Halifax for the start of the 1902-03 season. Halifax soon converted him into a centre whose selfless play contributed greatly to the club carrying off the Cup and League double in his first season. The following season "Wax" was in the team that retained the Challenge Cup and so joined Batley's Wattie Davies as the only Welshmen to win Challenge Cup Winners' medals in their first two seasons in the game. Williams was also the first Welshman to appear in a Northern Union Yorkshire Cup Final when he figured in the inaugural final of 1905 at Bradford Park Avenue when Halifax went down to Hunslet.

"Wax " moved to Rochdale Hornets in 1907 but had already been joined at Thrum Hall by another Welsh Williams in the shape of Billy (W.J.) Williams. Billy came up from Pontypool and proved to be a brilliantly effective try-scorer. His entry to the game came at a crucial time in the development of the sport for in 1906-07 radical changes were made including the reduction of teams to thirteen players. A new play-the-ball rule was introduced, referees were allowed to play advantage and the law concerning knock-on was laid down in its present form. In fact a "whole new ball game", to use a modern expression, was created. The local Halifax reporter merely remarked that under the new rules *"the pace is a real cracker"*. Billy Williams turned out to be a real cracker too scoring a try on his debut against Huddersfield on September 1st, 1906 and a week later grabbing two magnificent touchdowns at Wakefield. His speed enabled him to score 25 tries in his first season whilst his fellow winger, Percy Eccles, a local boy, broke the club record in claiming 39.

It had been thought that the new rules would work to the disadvantage of the Halifax side which had been successful previously largely because its defence was virtually impenetrable. Such was not the case, however, as the team showed wonderful attacking qualities. The inspiration of the team derived from the telepathic half-back combination of Jimmy Hilton and Tommy Grey. Grey had joined the club from Swansea and was later to help forge an even greater team with Wagstaff and his blesséd band at Fartown. There were those who believed that the blue and whites' success in 1906-07 rested not on the creativity of Hilton and Grey nor even on the deadly finishing of Williams and Eccles for this was the "Year of the Black Cat", which had nothing to do with the Chinese calendar! The feline in question was one "Smut" who had taken up residence at Thrum Hall in November following which point Halifax embarked upon a run of seventeen games without defeat. It was the cat that got most of the credit and she was lionised by the press from one end of the country to the other. She became the subject for large sales of postcards and buttons and received a silver collar from the Black Cat Cigarette Company.

Smut's efforts apart, Halifax topped the league at the close of the 1906-07 campaign but were obliged to compete for the Championship, which in previous years would have been theirs by right, in the new top-four play-off. Keighley were beaten 9-4 in a hard-fought semi-final before Oldham were vanquished 18-3 in the first Championship Final. Williams missed the final and most of the following season, however, as a result of a serious knee injury sustained in the semi-final.

It was because of Billy Williams' temporary incapacity that another Welsh wing flew into Thrum Hall. Williams was a sprinter of some note but the man the Halifax board acquired to replace him had an exceptional pedigree in speed. Dai Thomas, a native of Aberdare, joined Halifax in November 1907 from Dewsbury for whom he had scored 40 tries in the previous season, a club record which still stands and is the oldest of all club try-scoring records. In his last match of that campaign (April 13th, 1907) he had scored eight tries against Liverpool City to rob Percy Eccles of his place at the top of the try-scoring list. That haul of eight tries has never been exceeded by any other Welsh player in the game's history and was a record for a league fixture until Huddersfield's Australian winger Ray Markham scored nine against Featherstone in 1935.

Dai Thomas

Thomas had been a Cardiff player before going north to Dewsbury but had made his name with Aberdare for whom he had scored 80 tries in two seasons. He was reckoned to be the fastest man playing in either Association or Rugby football and had quickly become *"the most marked player in the Union"*. At eighteen he was the Welsh 100 yards champion and had defeated J. White Elswich, the English champion, in a race over 130 yards for a prize of £100. He had also accounted for the Canadian champion over 100 yards. Whilst at Dewsbury he had become one of that select band of Welshmen to be awarded a Yorkshire cap (Billy Williams emulated Thomas in this respect).

Thomas scored tries in seven of his first eight games with Halifax and finished the season with 22 in 25 appearances, Two of the most notable were scored after wonderful passing movements against the New Zealanders who went down 9-4 at Thrum Hall on a "mud heap". One newspaper reported that *"the match was by no means of a drawing-room order. When players were tackled they knew about it"*. Nonetheless at the dinner given for the Colonials after the match they were told that *"they had played as gentlemen!"* The tour manager, A.H. Baskerville, the man responsible for introducing League to New Zealand, responded by saying that *"the Halifax team could be complimented upon the great fight they put up. It was a pleasure to watch their magnificent passing and he did not think he had witnessed such fine movements since he had seen Northern Union football"*.

The New Zealanders were also the opponents of Wales that season in the first International match played by the Welsh under professional rules. Dai Thomas was on the Welsh left wing for the great match which was played on New Year's Day, 1908 at his old stamping ground in Aberdare. A crowd of 20,000 assembled with the *"South Wales Daily News"* reporting that *"at any time the interest would naturally be great, but as many South Wales players have gone over to Northern Unionism abnormal interest centres in the event"*. Interest was all the more marked in Aberdare as it was from that club's alleged payment to amateurs that several professional clubs sprang up in the valleys around that time.

The *"South Wales Daily News"* match report declared:

> *"During a game brimful of excitement there was no unseemly incident . . . . . and the surprise was that considering the bone in the ground below the soft and slippery surface and the strenuousness of the players no serious injury occurred. The play of the New Zealanders was in contrast with their exhibition at Merthyr in the early part of their tour. Their forwards were again beaten in heeling, but in other places of the play they were very smart, and in combined passing movements they excelled any Welsh amateur pack, while in footwork and fast rushing their only equals in Wales are to be found at Llanelli".*

The game was *"without exaggeration a spectacular treat"* with Ebbw

Vale's full-back "Chick" (T.E.) Jenkins playing the game of his life. So good was his performance that it was described as *"worthy of a Bancroft"* in allusion to Swansea's great full-back Billy Bancroft, a man challenged only by J.P.R. Williams as the finest of all Welsh RU full-backs. The game was as close a struggle as could be imagined and it fell to Dai Thomas to be the first scorer for Wales in an international, his try levelling the match at 3-3. Wales won the match 9-8 with a very late try from Dai "Tarw" Jones, one of the greatest Welsh Union forwards of his day and winner of thirteen RU caps.

Dai Thomas' international career consisted of the first three games played by Wales, all of which took place in 1908, and he scored a try in each.

In season 1908-09 Thomas and Billy Williams formed the most deadly pair of wingers in the Northern Union, Williams being restored to fitness once more. Thomas went over for 34 tries in 39 games and Williams shattered Eccles' club record by crossing for 45 in 39 games. Including representative matches Williams scored 49 tries to set up a new record for the Northern Union which he held jointly with Wigan's Joe Miller who also scored 49 tries that season. Williams and Salford's Joe Hoskins (30 tries in 1897-98) are the only Welshmen to have held the record for tries in a season. Halifax lost only five of 34 league fixtures and finished second to Wigan in the table. The Yorkshire Cup and the Yorkshire League were won and Halifax were strongly favoured to emulate Hunslet's feat of the previous season in lifting All Four Cups but having to play their final six fixtures in only twelve days, including the semi-finals of the Cup and Championship, proved too much of a burden. Williams set up a club record by scoring six tries against Keighley on January 1st, 1909 and had a haul of five against Wakefield Trinity. Thomas' best performance was to score four tries against his fellow countrymen from Treherbert, whilst he and Tommy Grey were the Halifax try-scorers in a 12-8 victory over the first Australian touring side although the turning point in this match was said to have been the wonderful chase and tackle by Williams on Australia's greatest League hero, Dally Messenger.

Dai Thomas left Halifax for Hull Kingston Rovers for the 1909-10 season having scored 56 tries in 64 appearances. He later played for Salford, Dewsbury and Ebbw Vale and remarkably played for each of those clubs against Halifax in 1910-11. His first game for Salford saw him score four tries but his second against Halifax at Thrum Hall saw him sent off for kicking his erstwhile colleague Billy Williams. When Thomas retired from rugby he took up gold-mining in Canada.

Williams continued to run in the tries for Halifax becoming the first player to amass 100 tries for the club when he scored at Hull on September 3rd, 1910. It had only taken him 117 games to achieve this landmark. By the time he played his final game against Ebbw Vale in

April 1912 he had scored 113 in 148 appearances. Repeated knee injuries caused him to retire. He made four appearances for Wales against England grabbing three tries in a 39-18 triumph at Ebbw Vale in 1910, one of only three hat-tricks credited to Welsh Internationals.

Before Williams departed from the scene he was joined at Thrum Hall by another Welsh international winger in Will (W.T.) Davies whose transfer from Batley cost the club £130 in November 1910. Halifax also had to allow centre Tom Parker, formerly of Cardiff, to join Batley. At 5' 10 $^1/_2$" and 13 st 10 lbs Davies was a jumbo-sized winger at a time when most forwards did not boast such dimensions but he was elusive and quick on his feet. These qualities had been necessary for a different reason when he came north from Tredegar in 1903 as he had to avoid an irate father-in-law. Davies, from Blackwood, was reported to have *"carried his bride in triumph to the north"* like some latter-day Viking when he signed for Batley. His bride whom he wed at Newport Register Office was the daughter of a Reverend Jones who had not been informed of the union.

Davies had done well at Batley playing in 209 games in the course of which he collected 69 tries. His career at Halifax was short but sweet for in his first season he scored 19 tries in only 25 games. On February 18th, 1911 he equalled Billy Williams' record by notching six tries in a cup-tie against York (also landing a goal) and ten days later ran in four against Warrington.

The following season was an amazing one for Davies in representative terms. He began by scoring all four of Wales' tries in a 20-28 defeat by Australia at Ebbw Vale on October 7th, 1911. No other player has ever scored four tries for Wales. The accomplishment bordered on the miraculous.. At Goodison Park, Everton on October 25th, he scored a try for the Northern Rugby League which went down 16-3 to the Kangaroos. He followed this on November 8th by scoring two tries for Great Britain at Newcastle in the first test which was lost 19-10. On December 20th in Bristol he scored a try for Wales & West of England against the Aussies who won 23-3. Finally, playing for Wales against England at Oldham on January 20th, 1912 he scored the only Welsh try in a 31-5 reverse. Astonishingly he had played in five international class matches all of which had been lost but had scored nine tries – the sum total that his sides had obtained. Allowing for the fact that he had played alongside such dominating centres as Bert Jenkins and Harold Wagstaff, the performance remains mind-boggling.

Davies' 25 tries for the season were the most by a Welsh player but he faded from the scene less than a year after his greatest performances.

A successor was not long in arriving at Thrum Hall for Frank Williams of Swansea was lured to Halifax, reputedly for £200 in gold. Born in Birmingham on 20th December, 1890 but Welsh in every other respect, Frank Williams played for Wales at Cardiff Arms Park in the first ever schoolboy international against England. He joined Halifax for the

Frank Williams

start of the 1913-14 season and his career was severely curtailed by the Great War. He did have time and the talent, however, to play his way into the Welsh team that lost to England (12-16) at St. Helens in February 1914 after only 19 appearances in the Halifax first team. Playing alongside Bert Jenkins he scored two tries and followed this by scoring three in a tour trial at Leeds a few weeks later. These performances earned him a place on the 1914 tour of Australasia. Frank played in the second and third tests against Australia, the latter being the "Rorke's Drift" test and the most celebrated of all Anglo-Australian encounters. Williams was one of five Welshmen to figure in the epic match although there were considerably more Welshmen in the original Rorke's Drift. Stand-off was his Halifax colleague Stuart Prosser whilst Leeds' W.A. Davies filled the other wing berth. Percy Coldrick (Wigan), an ex-Union cap, and Huddersfield's Jack Chilcott were the Welsh members of the pack. The story has repeatedly been told of how the British, reduced at times to ten men, repulsed everything that the Aussies could throw at them to win the Ashes with a heroic 14-6 victory. Williams was one of the injured, damaging his leg in the opening minutes and eventually having to depart from the fray.

By the time the tourists arrived home the Kaiser's War had begun and, although he played for a short time after the Armistice, Williams' rugby career had seen its greatest glory. Frank Williams' involvement with Rugby League was to continue until he reached the biblical three score years and ten, however, first as trainer to Halifax and then as reporter of the club's deeds for the "Halifax Courier & Guardian" from which he retired as sports editor in 1960.

It must have been very gratifying for Frank Williams to chronicle the great achievements of the club he had served as a player for his career with the pen spanned 40 years during which time the Halifax club contested eight Challenge Cup Finals (five at Wembley). Among those players whose fortunes he followed were another pair of Welsh wingers who burned up the turf for the Thrum Hall faithful in the late 1930s and into the post-war years. The dynamic duo were Jim Bevan and Arthur Bassett.

Jim Bevan was an unknown when he first played for Halifax under the assumed name of "Hughes" at Liverpool Stanley on September 26th, 1936 and it was not until Friday, 13th November that he signed away his amateur status for a bargain £175. Friday 13th certainly was anything but unlucky for both parties in this case as the young man from Cwmavon became a record-breaking try-scorer for the club even though the war deprived him of the honours he deserved.

When Bevan joined Halifax they had just embarked upon a spending spree that was to bring players of star quality to the club and culminate in victory at Wembley in 1939. George Todd, the English international stand-off, had already been signed from Hunslet and on the day that Bevan played his first match at Thrum Hall against Oldham the

Wembley 1939 – Wales and the All Black. Charlie Smith, Halifax's Maori centre, bursts past Salford's Gus Risman with Jim Bevan in support. Also in view is Blaina-born scrum-half, Jack Goodall.

spot lights were not trained on the unsung Welshman. The game, played in a blizzard, was notable for the debut of the giant Maori centre Charlie Smith who had reputedly cost £1,250 to procure from Streatham & Mitcham. Bevan would have felt at home in the Halifax pack that day as it contained four Welshmen in George Baynham, Arthur Childs, Stan Sparkes and Ossie Griffiths but must have wondered whether he was playing for the Barbarians as his fellow three-quarters were an Englishman, and Irishman and a New Zealander whilst both half-backs were Cornishmen. Full-back Hubert Lockwood was the only Yorkshire-born back and he was soon to be temporarily displaced by one of the most famous names in rugby – the great Maori, George Nepia.

When the 1937-38 season dawned Bevan was unable to gain a first team place until October 30th when Oldham were again the opposition at Thrum Hall. Once again the eyes of the crowd were not fixed upon Jim as three expensive captures were being paraded for their debuts. Fred Tottey, an Australian winger, and test forwards Harry Field and Harry Beverley had cost the club a small fortune but were expected to deliver the goods. From that match on Bevan never looked back and his right wing partnership with Smith became part of Thrum Hall folk-lore. By the season's end Bevan's fleetness of foot and great opportunism had won him a place in Jim Sullivan's Rugby League party to tour France. He was also included in a similar short tour to France the following November but the war was to rob him of a chance to tour Australia in 1940.

In 1938-39 Halifax fitted the final piece into their expensive jigsaw when they secured the services of Wales' finest winger, Arthur Bassett from Cardiff. The Rugby League hit Cardiff hard that season for apart from Bassett they lost Eddie Watkins and Gwyn Williams to Wigan and Jim Regan and Alban Davies to Huddersfield. Born at Kenfig Hill, Bassett had begun his career at Aberavon from where he won the first of his six Welsh caps in 1934 before moving onto Cardiff in 1935 at the same time as his brother Jack, who was a British Lion in 1930 and had won 15 caps as a full-back whilst with Penarth. At Cardiff Arthur scored 99 tries in 101 appearances which was ample testimony to his terrific finishing skills. Halifax signed Bassett on January 11th, 1939 and his first game for the reserves drew 5,000 spectators to a fog-shrouded Thrum Hall.

It was clear from the start that Bassett was something out of the ordinary. He was a powerful, long-striding athlete who could take the most direct route to the line or get through by virtue of speed and swerve. Although his defence was fallible on occasions he was reliable when the chips were down. Most importantly he was a crowd-pleaser and had that touch of charisma inherent in all great players. He seemed to ooze class, had marvellous anticipatory powers and could score sensational tries from any part of the field. Of course, Halifax had to pay well for such quality and Bassett reputedly received £1,000 – probably the largest fee paid to a Union convert before the war.

Arthur Bassett

He could hardly have asked for a more demanding first team debut than he had – Leeds at Headingley on January 28th before 27,000 spectators. Moreover he was pitted directly opposite Eric Harris, the "Toowoomba Ghost", thought by many to be without a peer in contemporary Rugby League. Harris crossed for one try but the pair gave each other a tough time and Bassett would have his revenge before too long. He was soon running in spectacular tries for his new club, many of which were long range efforts often accompanied by a characteristic kick and chase. His most important touchdown came in the Challenge Cup semi-final when he again opposed Eric Harris at Odsal Stadium in a match witnessed by an English Rugby League record crowd of over 64,000. Early in the game Halifax worked a well rehearsed ploy which came off perfectly. From a scrum Jack Goodall lofted a kick to Bassett's wing. The Leeds defenders were completely non-plussed as Bassett took the ball in his stride almost as if he was receiving a pass and scored without opposition. Leeds never recovered and Jack Goodall, a scrum-half from Blaina, ran the game finishing Leeds off with a try straight through the scrummage.

Halifax had qualified to meet Salford in the Cup Final and Bassett appeared at Wembley in only his 18th first-class match. He and Bevan formed a devastating three-quarter line with Smith and Jack Treen, two of the biggest and strongest centres in the game. The final proved to be rather one-sided as Halifax stormed home 20-3 winners. All the three-quarters except Bassett scored but Treen was able to use the threat posed by Bassett as a glorious foil to put Todd in for the best try of the game. Bassett played all over Barney Hudson, Salford's Test star, while Bevan's try near the end showed him at his most effective taking Chadwick's kick through and side-stepping the defence to hammer the final nail in Salford's coffin.

The Second World War truncated Bevan's appearances over the six seasons war-time football to only 85 in the course of which he claimed 67 tries. Bassett fared even worse being limited to a mere 47 games (26 tries) for the club. Even so Bevan scored 24 tries in 28 games in 1940-41 to finish third behind his compatriot Emlyn Walters in the try-scoring lists and became the most successful try-scorer in the club's history when he passed Joe Riley's total of 117 on February 3rd, 1945. It had taken Riley more than 400 matches to compile his aggregate which Bevan exceeded in his 172nd appearance. Bevan had scored 131 tries in only 207 games when he retired in 1946. He had played in the Cup Finals of 1941 and 1942 at Odsal when Leeds beat Halifax on both occasions and in other major finals contested by Halifax during the war. Bassett had not been available for the 1942 Final but had played full-back in 1941.

Bassett played for Wales against England in 1939, 1945 and 1946 and won selection for Great Britain's 1946 tour of Australasia claiming 18 tries in only eleven games. His greatest performances were reserved for the second and third tests against Australia – tragically his only test matches. Playing alongside Gus Risman, Bassett showed that he had retained his killer instinct by running in five tries including a barn-storming hat-trick in the 14-5 victory at Brisbane in the second test. Two more touchdowns in the Ashes-clinching 20-7 triumph at Sydney merely underlined what delights the rugby fraternity had been deprived of by six years of war.

Arthur Bassett is remembered as one of the finest of Welsh wingers even though his ten year career at Thrum Hall was reduced to a paltry 109 matches and 64 tries. He retired from the game in April 1950 after playing loose-forward for a time with York.

The twin gods, Bevan and Bassett had not departed before another brilliant Welsh winger arrived on the scene in August 1945. This was Arthur Harper Daniels, born at Pontyberem on September 12th, 1923, who came to Halifax via Llanelli. Along with two other Llanelli signings, John Davies (full-back) and W.T. Pritchard (hooker), Daniels made his try-scoring debut in a 31-3 home victory over Swinton on August 25th, 1945. Despite holding the right wing berth for thirty games during his first season he appeared to lack that vital ingredient necessary to ensure success – pace. As a defender he was superb, safe in the tackle and an intelligent positional player. He was also resolutely set upon becoming a top winger and after missing practically the whole of the 1946-47 season when he was serving overseas, Daniels set about improving his style, rhythm and speed. He succeeded admirably ridding himself of the habit of lowering his head when nearing a tackler which tended to negate his natural swerve. Always supremely fit, his speed improved to the point where he could claim justifiably to be the game's top British winger in the early 1950s, an era when the outstanding wings were men such as Brian Bevan, Lionel Cooper, Brian Nordgren and Peter Henderson – all Australians or New Zealanders. Apart from possessing most of the qualities required of a potent winger one of his favourite moves was the short kick over the tackler which he could execute so precisely that he could gather the ball before it came to earth. Many a try emanated from this simple manoeuvre.

When Daniels joined Halifax the team was struggling and continued to do so until 1949 when anther Welshman of Messianic qualities transformed a team of old stagers, has-beens and a few promising youngsters into a side that reached Wembley from 25th place in the league table and the following season led them to the promised land of the top four. This miracle-worker, prophet and man-of-action had also come north from Llanelli. A native of Llangennech, Gareth Price had been enticed to Leeds in 1938 for a consideration of £400. Halifax paid Leeds more than six times that figure in February 1949 for the tough-tackling, inspirational centre and they got more than their money's worth. Price had been capped 11 times as a centre for Wales as a League player and Daniels could have not asked for a better partner.

Wembley 1954.
Arthur Daniels prepares to receive from Tommy Lynch. Warrington winger Stan McCormick wonders what to do next.

No-one, except perhaps the players themselves and their mothers, ever dreamt that the Halifax team of 1949 would reach Wembley but against all the odds they battled through to meet Bradford Northern, whose second home the Empire Stadium had become. Arthur Daniels played his part scoring the only tries as Halifax beat Swinton 5-0 in the second round and Oldham 7-2 in the third before Huddersfield with their galaxy of stars were obliterated after a titanic struggle at Odsal in the semi-final. The bubble burst for Halifax as they lost 12-0 in the final before a crowd of 95,000, a record world-wide for Rugby League.

Daniels had forced his way into the Welsh team by February 1949 when he scored a debut try in a 14-10 defeat of England at Swansea. It was the first of 13 Welsh caps and although he only finished on the winning side in three of those internationals he took his chances so well that he scored nine tries and shares with Alan Edwards the distinction of scoring most tries for Wales. Edwards played five more internationals than Daniels, however, and arguably with stronger Welsh teams. Daniels also played for a Welsh XIII against a British Empire XIII in Llanelli in 1951. He scored a try playing outside Gareth Price and it must have given the pair great satisfaction to turn out in the town that bred them. In 1955 in Nantes Daniels and Billy Boston were an unlikely centre pairing for a Welsh XIII against France 'B'. It was Daniels' last appearance in the scarlet jersey of his country and he scored his customary try.

Daniels displayed such outstanding form in 1949-50 (34 tries in 37 appearances for Halifax) that he was an automatic choice for the 1950 tour of Australasia. Unfortunately it was an unmitigated disaster for Daniels, who was expected to be one of the test wingers. It started promisingly enough as he collected a hat-trick at Perth in the opening match when the tourists overran Western Australia 87-4. His second game, at Newcastle, saw him suffer a leg injury which cost him a place in the first test. At Kempsey against North Coast in his third game catastrophe struck for his collar-bone was fractured. By the time it healed the tour was almost over and he had been restricted to a mere five appearances from which he collected five tries. On the evidence of his performance at Woollongong after returning from his collar-bone injury when he scored two wonderful tries after combining with scrum-half Tommy Bradshaw, the Australian critics felt that the tourists had been cruelly deprived of their best winger.

It was not until the first test against Australia at Headingley in October, 1952 that Daniels found himself playing in a Great Britain jersey. He and Jack Evans, the Hunslet full-back, were the only Welshmen included in the side. The British had a fairly easy passage winning 19-6 and Arthur had a dream debut. He scored the final British try after fielding a poorly judged kick by Clive Churchill, the Australian full-back and captain. He evaded left-winger Brian Carlson, before side-stepping Noel Pidding, the other Aussie winger who was attempting to cover

Dai Bevan

before touching down near the corner for a try so spectacular that he was mobbed (uncharacteristically for those times!) by his enthusiastic team-mates. Retained for the second test at Swinton, which the British won 21-5 to wrap up the series, Daniels' luck deserted him as he sustained a splintered ankle bone which kept him out of the final test. Returning to club football with Halifax in December worse was to follow as he received a broken arm in the Christmas 'Day derby with Huddersfield and he played no more rugby that season. Arthur was captain of the team and his injury prevented him from leading out his men in the Championship Final of 1953.

Halifax did have a Welsh winger in that Championship Final, however, in Terry Cook, formerly of Pontypool and Cardiff. Cook had won Union caps against Scotland and Ireland in 1949 whilst with Cardiff for whom he scored 44 tries in 71 matches. He had joined Halifax for £2,000 in August 1950 but retired three years later aged only 26. His League career comprised 102 games and 49 tries for Halifax – not the best of Welsh bargains the club ever made. He won four Welsh RL caps.

Daniels returned for the 1953-54 campaign which was a momentous one for his club. Half-way through the season he was joined by another Welsh winger in Dai Bevan who was secured from Wigan after previously serving Belle Vue Rangers. Bevan, a native of Tonypandy, was very quick but more noted for a cast-iron defence. Whilst at Wigan he had twice been capped for Wales and once for Great Britain. He had in fact been the man who stepped in for the injured Daniels for the final test against Australia in 1952. He was a good man when the going got hot.

Halifax won the Yorkshire League and topped the league table in 1953-54. They also fought their way through to the Challenge Cup and Championship Finals facing Warrington in both. History records how the teams fought out the first drawn (4-4) final at Wembley although Halifax's dual Welsh International full-back Tuss Griffiths could have prevented a replay if his late penalty had passed a foot inside the upright rather than a foot outside. The replay at Odsal drew a world record crowd of 102,569 to its vast bowl as Warrington secured the trophy with an 8-4 victory. Many believed that Arthur Daniels scored a legitimate try almost on time. It was Daniels who leapt for a kick from scrum-half Stan Kielty which he caught over the "Wire" line and fell to earth for what may have proved a cup-winning try but the referee decreed that the ball was not grounded. Three days later at Maine Road, Manchester, Daniels again picked up a loser's medal as Warrington beat the blue and whites 8-7 in the Championship Final although Halifax scored the game's solitary try through ex-Neath forward, John Thorley. It would have been scant consolation for Daniels when after these heart-breaking defeats he scored a hat-trick against Warrington when the two teams met a few weeks later in Belfast and Halifax won 34-15 and repeated the dose the next day in Dublin with a 23-11 victory with Daniels scoring again.

Arthur Daniels (left) with Alvin Ackerley and Tuss Griffiths.

In 1954-55 Daniels finally got a cup-winners medal when Halifax defeated Hull 22-14 in a ferocious Yorkshire Cup Final at Headingley. Daniels set Halifax on their way soon after half-time when Kielty came round the blind-side of a scrummage and served the winger who nipped between two Hull defenders to put Halifax 12-4 ahead. Hull fought back to 12-9 before Kielty and Lynch put Daniels over again for the crucial score.

1955-56 was another great but ultimately disappointing season for Halifax and Daniels. In November Halifax and Hull met once again in the Final of the Yorkshire Cup at Odsal. The game was a replay following a 10-10 draw in an ugly match at Headingley where Halifax had let slip a ten point advantage. In the replay Halifax led 2-0 with never the vestige of a try from either side when Griffiths kicked for touch deep into Hull territory. The ball never reached touch for the Hull full-back just reached it before it went out of play flicking it infield behind him and expecting to gain possession. He hardly had time to turn, however, for Daniels was there like a bat out of hell hacking the ball on before falling on it in triumph for the only try of the day and sealing a 7-0 victory for Halifax.

Ten days later Daniels was back on the wing for Great Britain against New Zealand at Odsal sharing in a 27-12 series-clinching win. At the season's end he had scored 34 tries for the club which had won the Yorkshire League Championship. The team had also reached the Challenge Cup and Championship Finals as they had two years before. If they played up to form there was a possibility that All Four Cups would grace the Thrum Hall board room. Unfortunately St. Helens rose to the occasion at Wembley winning 13-2 and Daniels collected his third runners-up medal. The parallels with 1954 continued as the Championship final at Maine Road once again resulted in a one point defeat as Hull gained revenge for their Yorkshire Cup Final reverses winning 10-9 with a last minute penalty after Halifax had scored three tries to wipe out an 8-0 deficit. Daniels scored a try from a Kielty-Lynch manoeuvre but had earlier made a costly error in passing straight to Hull's scrum-half Finn whose resulting try had given Hull their eight points lead.

Daniels was fortunate to play alongside two great centres whilst a Thrum Haller – firstly with his compatriot Price and from 1952 to 1956 with Tommy Lynch. Lynch was an All Black from Canterbury who had played in three tests against the Wallabies in 1951 and he had cost Halifax a RL record fee of £5,000. He and Daniels seemed to have a telepathic understanding. Their exchanges down the right wing, their feints, scissor movements and sleight of hand mystified countless opponents who often had not a clue as to who actually had the ball. As a double-act they were something to behold and they are still rarely referred to separately. In all they appeared together as a partnership in 142 matches scoring 185 tries (Lynch 89, Daniels 96).

Daniels left Jim Bevan's record aggregate of tries way behind before he left Halifax for Bradford Northern in 1957 but his own record of 215 tries for the club was already being eroded by an even more prolific Welshman.

ARTHUR DANIELS' PLAYING RECORD FOR HALIFAX

	GAMES	TRIES	GOALS	POINTS
1945-46	30	7	1	23
1946-47	1	—	—	—
1947-48	30	5	—	15
1948-49	41	18	1	56
1949-50	37	34	—	102
1950-51	32	21	—	63
1951-52	39	28	—	84
1952-53	15	12	—	36
1953-54	45	28	—	84
1954-55	38	25	—	75
1955-56	46	34	1	104
1956-57	23	3	—	9
TOTALS	377	215	3	651

All first-class matches:

	463	268	3	810

Johnny Freeman stood six feet tall and weighed around 12$\frac{1}{2}$ stones and he was death to full-backs. He scored almost 300 tries for Halifax, was probably the world's deadliest winger at his peak and yet never got an international cap. He had the great misfortune to arrive on the Rugby League scene a couple of years after Mick Sullivan had taken a grip on the Great Britain left-wing spot and the teak-tough Sullivan held the position almost until his dotage. As in other aspects of life possession was nine-tenths of the law. In any other era Freeman would have won a bag full of caps.

A Cardiffian, Johnny Freeman started his rugby career at South Church Street School in the same team as Billy Boston. Stand-off for that side was Johnny's cousin, Joe Erskine, who was to become British Heavy-weight boxing champion. All three graduated to the Cardiff International Athletic Club, alias the Kyaks, and it was there that he drew upon himself the attentions of the Halifax club for whom he signed in December 1954. Johnny was ear-marked as a likely partner in the centre for Tommy Lynch and it was in that position that he made his debut at Thrum Hall on December 4th, 1954 against Wigan and his old friend Boston. Freeman and his winger Dai Bevan ensured that Billy was kept off the score-sheet for a change but Wigan won 6-2. New Year's Day saw

Johnny Freeman

Johnny on the left-wing for the first time but Leeds spoilt the Halifax festivities by winning 9-5 at Thrum Hall. The following week it was back into the centre at Dewsbury with Johnny scoring two tries and landing a long-range penalty goal to cap an outstanding exhibition of centre play that earned him a standing ovation at the game's conclusion.

Freeman's conversion from Union to League seemed to present him with no problems for he was clearly a "natural". If anything, he seemed over-confident, taking on defences as if he had all the answers and often he had. On February 5th, 1955, however, his first season came to an abrupt end as his shoulder was badly dislocated at Warrington. By the time he was fit again Halifax had secured another centre of outstanding promise in Geoff Palmer who immediately struck up a potent partnership with Lynch. It was not until the New Zealanders visited Thrum Hall on September 17th that Freeman was given another first-team appearance. In a memorable game Freeman played the leading part. Halifax trailed 6-5 shortly after half-time when their trio of Welsh three-quarters sprang into action. Bevan fielded a Kiwi kick and unleashed Freeman on a dazzling diagonal run in which he baffled three New Zealanders before working a scissors with Daniels who crossed for a glorious try. Well into the final quarter, however, Halifax faced a seven point deficit before Freeman latched on to a wild pass fifty yards out and with a magnificent burst left the Kiwis standing to score at the corner. Griffiths' touch-line conversion set up dramatic ending with Tommy Lynch scoring the winning try against his fellow country-men in the dying minutes to see Halifax home 18-17.

In his next game against Castleford Freeman scored one of the finest tries ever scored at Thrum Hall. Breaking through at a terrific pace, he disposed of one defender with an outrageous dummy before swerving away from two grasping opponents and embarked on a searing run which took him in a wide arc to the posts for a score which almost brought the main stand down. Scoring tries, even of such a sensational nature, failed to secure him a regular place in the Halifax team and he had to content himself with filling in for Lynch or Palmer when injured or unavailable. By March 1956, however, he had ousted Bevan from the left-wing and his season's work had brought him 21 tries including one in the Championship Final against Hull. He had also played in Halifax's disappointing Cup Final defeat by St. Helens at Wembley in only his 25th first-class match. He had been reduced to a limping passenger, however, after colliding with a photographer.

Halifax slumped from their accustomed exalted position in 1956-57 as their great team began to disintegrate but Freeman went from strength to strength. Billy Williams' club record came under threat as Freeman simply got better and better. In the period between December 8th and February 9th he ran in 23 tries in 10 matches. Scoring all three Halifax tries in a 25-9 defeat at Wigan on March 23rd he equalled Williams' record of almost half a century. Incidentally, this was one of only two occasions when an opposition winger went past Billy Boston for a hat-trick. Freeman finally smashed the record with a brace of tries against the French champions, Albi at Thrum Hall on April 13th.

Back in the swirling mists of time Huddersfield's Australian winger, the diminutive Abe Rosenfeld established Rugby League's record total for tries in a season with a phenomenal eighty. That record has rarely been in jeopardy but it was in 1957-58 when Johnny Freeman was nearing his peak. His try tally for the first twenty games of that campaign ran:

1,2,3,1,3,1,2,0,3,2,2,0,1,5,3,2,2,0,3,2

He had scored no less than 38 tries in those 20 matches, was virtually impossible to contain and seemed to score almost every time he received a pass. To use the modern expression, he was playing out of his skin. When Rosenfeld had set his record back in 1913-14 he amassed his eighty tries in 42 matches so Freeman was well on course and improving all the time. Rosenfeld was also a member of probably the greatest of all Rugby League sides. Freeman could not claim that, even though his team would win the Yorkshire Championship that season. A hat-trick at Doncaster on November 16th brought him his 100th try. It had only taken him 86 matches. The *"Rugby League Gazette"* issued its world-ratings and bracketed Freeman and Australia's Ian Moir as the world's leading wingers. Not even death and taxes were a surer bet than Johnny's inclusion in the 1958 Australasian tour party. Then, four days before Christmas, everything went horribly wrong as he was badly injured scoring his second try in a 36-7 victory over Batley at Mount Pleasant. His injuries put him out of the tour and out of the game for a year.

At the time of his injury Johnny had gathered 109 tries in 91 matches and his rate of scoring was continuously accelerating. One can only surmise what records would have gone by the board had he not suffered such a cruel twist of fate.

By the time he had re-established himself on the Thrum Hallers' left flank in 1959 Halifax had become a team struggling to break away from the middle of the table. Even so he continued to pile up the tries although the rate was not quite so frenetic as of yore. By 1963 Halifax were beginning to come good again and Freeman contributed 22 tries as the Yorkshire Challenge Cup and the Eastern Championship were taken in 1963-64. A hat-trick against York on October 5th took him past Arthur Daniels' club record of 215 tries. The following season Halifax lifted the Rugby League Championship defeating St. Helens 15-7 in the final. Only Trevor Lake, Wigan's Rhodesian winger, scored more tries than Freeman during the season. After appearing in another Championship Final in 1966 Freeman played on into 1966-67 season making his last appearance in a drawn game at Oldham on March 27th, 1967.

No British player has scored as many tries (291) as Johnny Freeman and still not earned an international cap. Countless inferior wingers have played for Wales and Great Britain. For those who were privileged to see Freeman at his most devastating that fact amounts to sacrilege yet it is only an accident of history. There were no Welsh international teams during his career and Mick Sullivan proved indestructible having got into the test team before Freeman entered the sport. Johnny did in fact play for a Welsh XIII against France in Toulouse in 1963 but it was not accorded the status of a full international and no caps were awarded.

Freeman scored an amazing number of tries bearing in mind that, apart from the beginning and end of his career, he played in a mediocre team and had a large variety of centre partners. His combination with Geoff Palmer in the early stages of his career was exceptionally dangerous, however, and towards the end he enjoyed a fruitful alliance with the youthful Colin Dixon.

Freeman's greatest asset was his scorching pace. No-one could allow him half a yard and expect to catch him. Once away the most an opponent could expect was to see his dust. With the ball tucked under his left arm he would employ a juddering hand-off to anyone attempting to tackle him on the touch-line. A full-back left alone to face Freeman might as well have waved him on for his cause was lost. Freeman could beat him on the outside or the inside or would kick past the poor man to start an unequal race. He had any number of ways of beating a man. Often enough it seemed that a full-back would take him but just as he got to him Freeman would somehow lengthen his stride at the point of impact and leave his opponent floundering. A player who did get close enough to touch him would often find himself so deceived by his change of pace that he would be thrown off balance and lack the strength to hold on to the flying Freeman. Many of Freeman's tries were scored in the grand manner – length of the field sprints, serpentine spurts through clusters of tacklers, long distance interceptions, impossible dashes down the touch-lines – and he was one of those players who had the crowd on tenter-hooks whenever he had possession, for a try was always on even if it was not!

There will always be a welcome for Welsh wingers in the Halifax hill-side especially if they are anything like as good as Johnny Freeman.

JOHNNY FREEMAN'S PLAYING RECORD FOR HALIFAX

	GAMES	TRIES	GOALS	POINTS
1954-55	4	2	1	8
1955-56	22	21	5	73
1956-57	45	48	9	162
1957-58	20	38	—	114
1958-59	16	9	—	27
1959-60	34	25	—	75
1960-61	40	29	—	87
1961-62	33	19	—	57
1962-63	43	23	—	69
1963-64	38	22	—	66
1964-65	34	28	—	84
1965-66	42	18	—	54
1966-67	25	8	—	24
TOTALS	396	290	15	900

All first-class matches:

	GAMES	TRIES	GOALS	POINTS
	398	291	15	903

Chapter 10

Four for the flanks

Wales has produced literally dozens of top class wingers for the Rugby League. Their names are writ large in the annals of the game and their glory endures. Men such as Boston, Ring, Freeman, Roy Francis, Wattie Davies, Bassett, Morley and Daniels are dealt with elsewhere in these volumes. Other exceptionally fine wingers have been omitted whose exclusion may offend their admirers but no slight is intended. St. Helens devotees, for example, have down the years thrilled to the exploits of Stuart Llewellyn, Frank Wilson and Roy Mathias, each of whom in his own different ways crossed for over two hundred touchdowns. Bradford has welcomed Welsh flyers such as Fred Cooper, probably the fastest man around in the earliest years of the Northern Union and in the 1960s Berwyn Jones, the great athlete and certainly the fastest Welsh player by track times of any era. Jones, a former Union player with Rhymney, astounded both the athletics and rugby fraternities when he turned professional with Wakefield Trinity in 1964. He proved Trinity's gamble was no gimmick by becoming a test player and won selection to tour Australasia in 1966. The list of superb Welsh wings is seemingly endless – Frank Evans (Swinton), Malcolm Davies (Leigh and Bradford), Freddie Smart (Huddersfield and Wakefield), Emlyn Walters and Des Case (Bradford), Alf Francis and Emlyn Gwynne (Hull), Llew Llewellyn (Ebbw Vale), Ray Glastonbury (Workington), Les Williams (Hunslet), Reg Lloyd (Keighley and Castleford), Roy Lambert (capped as a League player from Neath!). and so on, right down to modern specialists like Cambriani, Camilleri, Prendiville and Ford.

The careers of four outstanding wingmen depicted below, however, should find favour with all connoisseurs of the highest arts of wing play. A combined total of tries in excess of 1,200 is a powerful testimony to their right to be ranked among the greats of their species.

Alan Edwards
(Aberavon RU, Salford RL, Dewsbury RL, Bradford Northern RL)

By the time he was twenty-one Alan Edwards' test career was over – the Second World War saw to that – but by the time he was twenty-two he had won all the major prizes open to him. Victory at Wembley in 1938, a Championship winners' medal, a Lancashire Cup winners' medal and one for the Lancashire League, seven test matches with half-a-dozen tries thrown in, eight Welsh RL caps as Wales took the international championship in three consecutive seasons and selection for the 1936 tour to

Frank Evans (ex-Llanelli and Wales RU wing).
Record try scorer (197) for Swinton 1921-31.

Les Williams (Hunslet and ex-Cardiff).
A superb winger who won 7 Union caps and 15 League caps for
Wales (1949-53).

Ray Glastonbury (Workington Town)
League's top try scorer 1962-63.

Australasia as the youngest player ever to win that honour.

Edwards was certainly a champion and one of the game's greatest left-wingers and his achievements over fifteen seasons in the sport were staggering. Yet when he came into the game he hardly looked the part. Skinny and pallid, his slight frame bore just over ten stones and even by the end of his career he struggled to reach 11 $^1/_2$ stones. Yet he was a scourge to the stoutest of defences and stood out in an era of outstanding wingers.

Writing in 1969, Eddie Waring, whose way with words was not always wayward, described Edwards most fittingly thus:

> "*Clichés don't always fit the player. In the case of Alan Edwards most of them did. He did 'thunder' down the wing. He could side-step 'off a penny'. And he ran like a 'hare'.*"

Alfred Drewry of *"The Yorkshire Post"* wrote of Edwards in 1950:

> "*When he sets off to run, lips in a tight, grim line, there is determination and antagonism in every movement of his lean, taut frame. It is a legacy of his early days. When Lance Todd spotted him playing for Aberavon in 1935 his weight was only 10st 2lbs, and to score tries he just had to give everything he had*".

Edwards certainly did give everything when he set his sights on the try-line. If it was a case of belting hard and straight for the corner Edwards flew like an arrow. Pursuit was invariably futile, a waste of energy for those optimistic enough to attempt to stop his flight. If the way was barred his tremendous speed was aided and abetted by an outrageous side-step off either foot. When all else failed he could make the line through sheer determination. Edwards was one of those players who really "wanted" the ball and once he had it, he was likely to do something spectacular with it.

Wales certainly lost one of its brightest potential stars when Salford signed the nineteen-year-old Edwards on September 16th, 1935. Born at Kenfig Hill on May 15th, 1916, Edwards made brief appearances for Maesteg and Bridgend before becoming established in senior rugby with Aberavon where he was worthily treading in the hallowed footsteps of Johnny Ring. By the time he was eighteen he was appearing in the Welsh trials opposite another great ex-Aberavon and future League star in Arthur Bassett, physically a much more intimidating specimen than the frail youngster from Kenfig Hill.

There was to be no Welsh RU cap for Edwards, however, although he would appear in six war-time services internationals for Wales against England as a Union player. As a League player he would win 18 caps over a period of 13 years and no man would score more than the nine tries he registered for his country, although Arthur Daniels would equal his tally.

Having joined Salford he made his debut for the Red Devils at

Alan Edwards

Broughton Rangers on September 21st, 1935 and by the season's close had figured in the Championship-winning team as Salford snatched a pulsating late victory over Warrington (13-11) in the final. His impact had been stunning enough to catapult him into the Welsh team and even more sensationally into the 1936 tour party to Australia. At the time of his selection he was still nineteen and the youngest man ever to be so honoured. Alec Murphy in 1958 and Garry Schofield in 1984 have since beaten Edwards' youthfulness in this respect.

Many thought that Edwards was still sharp enough to be selected again in 1946 for he was still a great player but he had to be content with a solitary trip down-under. On that 1936 tour Edwards fulfilled all expectations finishing as the top try-scorer with 21 in 16 matches. He and his club colleague Barney Hudson kept such great wings as Jack Morley and Stan Smith out of the test sides with Edwards appearing in all five tests. His first experience of test match action was not too happy as Britain were hammered 24-8 by Australia at Sydney. In the vital second test, however, Edwards proved the match-winner. Playing opposite Archie Crippin, the Kangaroos' own prodigy at only nineteen, Edwards scored at the corner after ten minutes to give the tourists the opening score. He was then denied a try after a glorious interception when the referee ruled no try after he slid over the line. Crippin's sensational seventy yard try following a Risman error levelled the scores at 5-5 before a Salford Welsh combination won the test for the British. Emlyn Jenkins, the stand-off, was the architect flighting an inch-perfect kick to the corner for Edwards to roar onto fractionally before Crippin. Risman converted from touch and the series was squared. With victories over Australia in the remaining test and over the Kiwis in both New Zealand tests both series were won. Edwards was, however, only to play in one more test series, appearing in the second and third tests of the home series against the Aussies in 1937. His two tries in the second test at Swinton were one of the crucial factors in a 13-3 victory enabling the home country to retain the Ashes.

In club football Edwards was extraordinarily fortunate to play in hugely successful teams at Salford and Bradford Northern, and during the war at Dewsbury where he was often employed at centre in a star-studded three-quarter line. He was doubly blest to have as his centre partners two of the most accomplished men to have graced that position. In Gus Risman at Salford and Ernest Ward at Odsal, Edwards knew that his talents would be sublimely harnessed to their own. The two were artists in unleashing this greyhound of a winger at the most opportune moment and Edwards could be guaranteed to repay their generosity.

Whilst a Red Devil Edwards began to collect medals in earnest beginning with a winners' medal for Salford's 5-2 victory over Wigan in the Lancashire Cup Final but having to be content with a losers' medal for the 1938 final. Lancashire League medals came his way in 1936-37 and

Bradford Northern with the Challenge Cup 1949.
Welshmen abound. Frank Whitcombe holds skipper Ernest Ward by the left leg. To Whitcombe's right are
Ron Greaves (ex-Abertillery), Alan Edwards and Willie Davies.
On the extreme left is manager Dai Rees (ex-Abertillery R.U., Halifax R.L., Wales R.L.).

1938-39. In 1938 he appeared at Wembley in his first Challenge Cup Final helping Salford to defeat Barrow 7-4. The following year he was back at the Empire Stadium when his side lost heavily to Halifax. However, it was no fault of Edwards for he was far and away their best player enthralling the southerners with a series of spectacular but fruitless runs. A week later in the Championship Final against Castleford at Maine Road he scored what many regard as his finest try. Certainly it was one of the most important touchdowns he ever contrived. The game was eight minutes from its conclusion and Salford were striving might and main to wipe out Castleford's flimsy 6-5 lead but they were pinned in their own "25" when a scrum went down. Bert Day heeled to his compatriot Billy Watkins who handed on to Tom Kenny. Kenny parted to another Taff in right centre Gear, whose try the previous year had brought the Challenge Cup to the Willows. Three pairs of hands the ball had passed through but not an inch of ground had been gained. Gear weighed up the situation. Risman and Edwards were outside him but the Castleford spotters were closer than their own jerseys so the centre cross-kicked to the left flank well ahead of Edwards. The winger was into his stride immediately and was in possession of the ball in the blink of an eye, or so it seemed. But he still had more than half the length of the field to negotiate and he had to dispose of winger Bernard Cunniffe and centre Jimmy Robinson, who were covering like avenging angels and then there was dependable George Lewis, the full-back, to avoid. An extravaganza of side-step and swerve left them all clutching thin air and lucky to have got that much! The amazing thing about the try was the fact that Edwards had hardly deviated a foot or so in his headlong flight along the touch-line. It was a try fit to win a Championship.

Edwards appeared in no fewer than six Championship Finals in his career, twice with each of his clubs. His record in Challenge Cup Finals was even better for he graced seven, a record until Eric Batten appeared in his eighth with Featherstone in 1952. Batten had been Edwards' team-mate in three of those finals whilst a Bradford player. In 1942 Edwards had scored two tries as a guest for Leeds in their Cup Final victory over Halifax but the following year was scoring against Leeds for Dewsbury who lifted the trophy by winning a two-legged final 16-15 on aggregate. In 1945 he was guesting for Bradford Northern when they were defeated by Huddersfield 13-9 over two legs, figuring at centre to Batten in both games.

Bradford were so keen to have Edwards on a permanent basis that they paid Salford £700 for him on August 28th, 1946 although he was thirty by then. The Odsal club got three full seasons' service from Alan, seasons which saw Northern reach Wembley each time. In 1946-47 Edwards scored four tries in the rounds leading up to the final against Leeds. Northern won the Challenge Cup with an 8-4 victory but Edwards missed the final having dislocated a shoulder, his third such mishap that

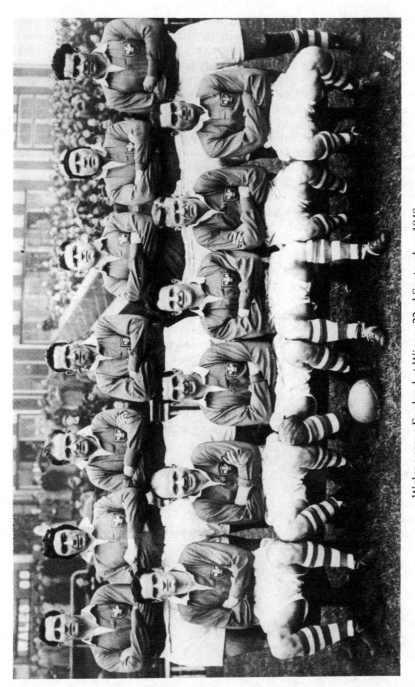

Wales versus England at Wigan, 22nd September, 1948.
Back: Ted Ward, W.J.D. Howes, Ike Owens, Charlie Staines, Elwyn Gwyther, Mel Meek, Dai Davies
Front: Stuart Llewellyn, Joe Mahoney, Dai Jenkins, Len Constance, Alan Edwards, Joe Jones.

season. The following season Northern won the Yorkshire League and were defeated by Warrington in the Championship Final. A week previously they had gone down 8-3 to Wigan in the Challenge Cup Final with Edwards scoring Bradford's only try.

In his last full season Edwards was going as strongly as ever and played a storming game in the 18-9 Yorkshire Cup Final victory over Castleford at Headingley. Twelve points from two tries and three goals was his considerable contribution to Northern's cause – no-one has ever scored more points in the final of this competition – but in scoring his second try he suffered another severe shoulder injury. Typically he was back in action by the time the Challenge Cup-ties of 1949 came round. Firing on all cylinders he ran in six tries in the cup run that took Northern to their third consecutive Wembley Final and he was there in his accustomed left-wing spot as Halifax were defeated 12-0 to pick up his fourth winners' medal from seven finals.

There were only to be another six first team games for Edwards. 1949-50 began well enough for the Welshman as he passed the land-mark of scoring 1,000 points with two goals at Keighley in the first match of the season. His last tries, a brace, were scored on August 31st, 1949 at Odsal against one of his former clubs, Dewsbury, but disaster struck at Warrington on September 7th when his ankle was fractured. Even so the gritty winger tried to return through the "A" team but was compelled to retire because of recurrent shoulder problems.

Records and limbs are made to be broken and so was the mould as far as Alan Edwards is concerned.

ALAN EDWARDS' PLAYING RECORD FOR SALFORD

	GAMES	TRIES	GOALS	POINTS
1935-36	28	21	—	63
1936-37	33	15	—	45
1937-38	32	21	—	63
1938-39	46	33	—	99
1939-40	26	20	—	60
1940-41	1	2	—	6
1945-46	33	17	29	109
TOTALS	199	129	29	445

ALAN EDWARDS' PLAYING RECORD FOR
BRADFORD NORTHERN

	GAMES	TRIES	GOALS	POINTS
1939-40	20	3	—	9
1944-45	16	6	—	18
1946-47	24	13	6	51
1947-48	36	36	2	112
1948-49	32	23	16	101
1949-50	5	2	9	24
TOTALS	133	83	33	315

All first-class matches:

	440	294	70	1,022

Maurice Richards
(Cardiff RU, Salford RL)

Unlike his great predecessor Edwards, Maurice Richards arrived at Salford as an acknowledged star of the Union game in both hemispheres. With nine Welsh caps and three for the Lions in South Africa on the 1968 tour and with a penchant for conjuring tries out of nothing, Richards was widely regarded as the world's top winger. When he signed for Salford on October 15th, 1969 he surprised everyone for most unusually it had been a case of Richards approaching the club rather than the reverse. The fee was variously reported as £7,000-£9,000. Whatever the cost, it was little enough for Maurice gave his club fourteen years of record-breaking service.

Apparently less aggressive than Edwards, Richards was no less effective. A graceful, elegant runner, Richards had a more robust physique than Edwards weighing a shade over 12 $^1/_2$ stones and standing an inch short of six feet. Moreover he was devilish fast and, like Edwards, he could side-step prodigiously both ways. He could also stop almost dead whilst at full throttle before generating instant acceleration – a most disconcerting manoeuvre for those trying to halt his majestic progress for they would suddenly find themselves on a collision course with thin air. When he entered League there were some misgivings about his tackling but he was soon being regarded as one of the great all-round wingers of his era. Although Richards scored many, many spectacular tries from deep positions he was never a flamboyant character, always appearing cool and unaffected. He simply got on with the job of scoring tries. His conduct was never less than exemplary.

A true son of the valleys, Maurice Charles Rees Richards was born

Maurice Richards

at Ystrad Rhondda on February 2nd, 1945 and educated at Tonypandy Grammar School from where he won Welsh caps as a centre. It was as a centre that he joined Cardiff for the 1963-64 season during which, as an eighteen-year-old, he faced Wilson Whinneray's awesome All Blacks before a crowd of 55,000 at the Arms Park. Richards made 171 appearances in the blue and black livery of Cardiff and scored 97 tries. Once he scored four tries against Gloucester and on the club's 1967 tour to South Africa bagged 19 points (3 tries, 5 goals), against Eastern Province.

Moving out to the wing, where his attacking brilliance could be given free rein, Maurice began to establish himself as one of the great Welsh wings. His first full cap was won on March 9th, 1968 against Ireland in Dublin and it must almost have been like playing in the Cardiff back division for on the opposite wing was Keri Jones, later to join Wigan, with the twin god-head at half-back in Barry John and Gareth Edwards, not to mention John O'Shea in the pack. The Cardiff presence counted for little, however, as the Irish won 9-6. In 1969 Wales were undefeated, winning the Championship and the Triple Crown with Richards appearing in every match and scoring six tries, four of which earned him immortality in Welsh eyes. The four came against England in the final match of the championship at Cardiff and equalled the Welsh record jointly held by Willie Llewellyn of Llwynypia, who scored four against the English in 1899, and by Cardiff's own Reggie Gibbs who had performed the feat against France in 1908. The last of his nine internationals was a 19-16 victory over Australia at Sydney in the summer of 1969. The last of his seven tries for Wales had been scored in the second test against New Zealand at Auckland during the same tour, a baffling individual effort in which his stuttering change of pace left Earl Kirton and Fergie McCormick for dead. McCormick effected a resurrection, however, to kick a record 24 points as the Welsh were crushed 33-12.

When Richards signed for Salford he was the fourth member of the 1968 British Lions South African tour party to turn professional. Apart from Keri Jones, his fellow Cardiff wing, Mike Coulman, the English RU forward had preceded him to the Willows and a couple of weeks before Richards went north his international centre partner, Keith Jarrett of Newport had thrown in his lot with Barrow.

Richards made his debut for Salford against an Alec Murphy inspired Leigh side fresh from thirteen successive victories. The date was October 15th, 1969 and Richards' appearance helped to draw a crowd of almost 12,000 to the Willows. Maurice did not score but impressed in a 15-5 victory. He scored his first try six days later in a Floodlit Trophy match against Castleford. Things happened quickly and within eight days of his debut he appeared for Wales, as centre to his old Cardiff colleague Frank Wilson, against France. Promotion to Welsh international Rugby League teams sometimes comes quickly. Jarrett had been selected to play against England before he had made his Barrow debut

but he had not been fit. Back in 1950 the St. Helens centre, Don Gullick, nephew of the dual international forward Percy Coldrick, played against England in only his seventh match, having won selection after a mere three outings.

Surprisingly, Maurice played only three times for Wales as a League player due largely to him declaring himself unavailable for representative rugby. Indeed very little was seen of Richards at international level. The only tests he played were two on the 1974 tour of Australasia when he was flown out as a replacement for the injured John Atkinson. The following year he declined to tour again with Wales in the World Championship tournament. His last international match was against England at Headingley in 1977 when Wales won possibly the dreariest of all international matches 6-2, a game when the wingers may as well have stayed at home.

His self-imposed exile from international participation could not detract from his wonderful service to Salford, although as a Methodist lay-preacher he did for a time struggle to reconcile himself to playing on Sundays. How some of his opponents wished he had not broken the sabbath!

Of course, Richards joined a very talented team for Salford had numerous outstanding players, particularly among the back division. When he joined the club the right wing berth was held down by Billy Burgess who was ultimately succeeded by Keith Fielding. It was therefore futile for the opposition to try and close down one wing for Salford had a tornado on each almost throughout Richards' career at Weaste. He was also fortunate enough to have as his centre on the left flank Chris Hesketh. Hesketh and Richards enjoyed a prolific partnership for almost a decade, and centres did not come much better than the gifted Hesketh.

Richards never played in a Challenge Cup Final but won numerous honours with Salford who lifted the First Division Championship in 1973-74 and 1975-76, the Lancashire Cup in 1972 and the Floodlit Trophy in 1974-75 as well as finishing runners-up in several other trophy tilts. Throughout the seventies Richards was consistently among the tries and topped the lists in Salford's Championship season of 1975-76 when he roared in for 37, four more than his nearest challenger, Keith Fielding. His value to the club was inestimable and even when the glory days were over Maurice was there faithfully piling up the tries. On September 5th, 1982 in a Lancashire Cup-tie at Wigan Maurice scored his 293rd try for Salford to surpass the record of Barney Hudson, the block-busting winger who had scored 292 between 1928 and 1946. A month later (October 3rd) – appropriately enough in Cardiff against the Blue Dragons – he scored the 300th try of his professional career and, into the bargain, broke Bert Day's record for the most appearances with Salford. It was a real Welsh rarebit – a Welshman beating a fellow Welshman's record in the Welsh capital.

Maurice Richards served both codes of rugby nobly. If he had a fault it was that he lacked a bit of devil but try telling that to all those opponents who found him a big enough nuisance without it. Over 300 tries tells its own story.

MAURICE RICHARDS' PLAYING RECORD FOR SALFORD

	GAMES	TRIES	GOALS	POINTS
1969-70	26	13	27	93
1970-71	42	23	2	73
1971-72	44	35	—	105
1972-73	47	38	—	114
1973-74	30	18	—	54
1974-75	45	28	3	90
1975-76	46	37	—	111
1976-77	28	23	—	69
1977-78	34	22	—	66
1978-79	33	10	—	30
1979-80	36+2 subs	10	—	30
1980-81	37	14	—	42
1981-82	39	20	—	60
1982-83	8	5	—	15
1983-84	1	1	—	4
TOTALS	496+2 sub	297	32	956

All first-class matches:

	GAMES	TRIES	GOALS	POINTS
	509+2 sub	302	32	971

Clive Sullivan
(Hull RL, Hull Kingston Rovers RL, Oldham RL, Doncaster RL)

To play top-class Rugby League for twenty-three seasons, appear in well over 600 matches and to pillage opposing sides for more than 400 tries constitutes an amazing career record. To achieve these feats after being told by doctors on more than one occasion that any prospect of participating in even the gentlest of activities was out of the question, that the very act of walking might be beyond him, borders on the miraculous. This was the experience of Clive Anthony Sullivan, a man who overcame the most debilitating of injuries, survived repeated encounters with the surgeon's scalpel and rose from the depths of despair to become one of Rugby League's most lionised ambassadors, captain of his country and a byword for courage and skill.

Clive Sullivan pursued by Berwyn Jones.

To catalogue the injuries suffered by Clive Sullivan to knees, thighs, shoulders and feet which all required major surgery from his early teens, when he was told he would never be able to walk normally again, through to his twenties would require several paragraphs. Another paragraph would be required to itemise the dreadful injuries he suffered in a car crash in 1963 when he was twenty years-old. Just about everything that could be broken had been and everything that could be torn was. After such an horrendous accident he was told he was lucky to be alive never mind worrying about when he would get back onto the rugby pitch. That was out of the question – again.

Fate seemed to have it in for Clive Sullivan. He should have been called Job for the heavenly powers tested his childhood resolve to become a great rugby player almost as often and as cruelly as they did his biblical predecessor. In the end both Job and Clive Sullivan triumphed but how they had to endure!

Sullivan's bravery and determination in the face of foul adversity have been recognised in other writings and need no further recounting here. Suffice it to say that Clive's successes owed nothing to luck but everything to an unquenchable spirit and an innate talent.

Clive Sullivan hailed from Splott in Cardiff where he was born in 1943. His boyhood hero was Billy Boston but his hopes of emulating the great Wigan wing star were crippled, literally, by the time he was thirteen. Clive had begun his rugby playing at Herbert Thompson Secondary Modern School, Ely and had represented Cardiff Schools against Bridgend in the company of Colin Dixon, another future Rugby League world-beater and a life-long friend and rival. That, however, had been the summit of his achievements in schoolboy rugby for at that point his world was shattered when a thigh injury and resultant operation decreed that he should not play rugby again as a boy. Oddly enough, Clive joined the army at seventeen and was assigned to Billy Boston's former regiment, the Royal Signals at Catterick. As a soldier chance cast him back into rugby, despite misgivings and fears, and it was soon obvious that he had lost none of his talents. Rugby League scouts began to show an interest and he was invited to play a trial for Bradford Northern. Having seen him play in one "A" team match Northern decided he would never make it but Hull had more sense. He was invited to trial at the Boulevard and was thrown into the first team straightaway.

December 9th, 1961 was the occasion for Sullivan's debut in first-class League but interest was primarily centred on Wilf Rosenberg who was also making his debut on the right wing. Rosenberg, "the flying dentist", was a South African with five caps for the Springboks to his credit. He was to become a fine League winger in his own right and that day against Bramley ran in two tries. But it was the young Sullivan on the opposite flank who really took the eye, hurtling in for a hat-trick and bringing the Threepenny Stand to the point of ecstasy with his final effort which began near his own line and involved a run during which he seemed to beat half the Bramley team. If the Hull directors had not signed Sullivan after that they would have been lynched.

Sullivan immediately came under the influence of Roy Francis, the Hull coach, who knew all there was to know about wing play. Roy, of course, was a fellow Welshman who had distinguished himself as a player at the Boulevard. Apart from Roy Francis, Sullivan was following in the footsteps of two other great Welsh wings at Hull. Alf Francis, a delightful, diminutive winger from Treherbert had joined Hull in 1910 and gone on to become one of the best wingers of the pre-Great War era despite the fact that he had been signed as a scrum-half. He toured Australasia in 1914 and scored 167 tries for the Airlie Birds, a record which Sullivan would later better. Alf Francis retired in 1921 to be replaced by Emlyn Gwynne, formerly of Mountain Ash and Swansea. Gwynne gave Hull nine seasons' service, running in 108 tries in 283 matches and emulated Francis by touring in 1928.

Clive Sullivan more than upheld the Welsh wing tradition at Hull. A club record of 250 tries is ample testimony to the effectiveness of his work on the Hull wings – he played with equal facility on either left or right. Clive was built for speed at 5' 11" and around 12 $1/_2$ stones and those spindly, glistening legs, which drew so much surgical attention, carried him effortlessly and gracefully past multitudes of frustrated tacklers. Sullivan was a real sprinter, poetry in motion and speed was certainly the deadliest weapon of his armoury. If there was space on the outside Sully could be gone in a flash and it was testimony to his fitness and ability to retain his fleetness that he hardly ever played in any other position than wing even at the age of forty. In later years he developed the habit of dipping his shoulder into opponents to compensate for the inevitable decline in that blistering pace that he generated for so long. Although Clive was undoubtedly one of the game's most polished attacking wingers his reputation was enhanced by his fail-safe defensive qualities. A master of the cover tackle, Sullivan was likely to pop up in the most improbable of situations on the field to do more than the share of the tackling expected of a winger. His roving tendencies stood him in good stead on being given the captaincy of the test team when his peculiarly ubiquitous brand of wing play and personal example gave the lie to the belief that wingers should not skipper Rugby teams.

In his first three seasons in the irregular black and white hoops of the Hull club Clive underwent three knee operations, was almost killed in that horrific car smash and was posted to trouble-torn Cyprus. His appearances were restricted to a mere 32 during that period but 26 tries in a mediocre side indicated that he would make the grade providing his legs did not disintegrate. Sully played at the Boulevard for 13 seasons during which the club were not particularly successful. In all that time he only appeared in one cup final scoring a try in the 12-9 Yorkshire Cup

Final victory over Featherstone in 1969, Hull's first triumph in that competition for 46 years. Two years earlier Hull had met neighbours Hull K.R. in the final – losing by a point – but Clive had been forced to miss the game through one of his operations.

If the team was not a roaring success its Welsh winger certainly was. On April 15th, 1968 Clive scored seven tries in a 57-6 victory at Doncaster to erase the club record held by Alf Francis and in 1970-71 he ran in 33 tries to set a post-war club record. By the conclusion of the 1973-74 season he had scored more tries than any player in the club's history, had received a well deserved benefit, had made 17 test appearances, won five Welsh caps, made two trips down-under and had received the M.B.E. for his services to the sport. He was 31 and a living legend of League. Most mortals would have been happy to call it a day but not Clive Sullivan. Leaving the Boulevard was bad enough in the black and white eyes of the Hull Old Faithfuls but to cross the city and to don the red and white of Kingston Rovers was tantamount to treason but that is what Clive did.

Glorious though his career had been at Hull at a personal level it did not match the half-dozen years he spent with Rovers in terms of tangible rewards. In 1973-74, however, Rovers found themselves at the wrong end of the First Division and were relegated. Such a situation could not be tolerated. Rovers secured the services of two of the greatest names in the sport to help them out of the mire in Clive Sullivan and Neil Fox, even more of a veteran than Sully. The pair made their debuts in a 33-3 win at Doncaster on August 25th, 1974 and Rovers never looked like staying in the lower division, finishing runners-up to Huddersfield. Into the bargain they won a classic Yorkshire Cup Final victory over Wakefield Trinity with Clive scoring a try but having to retire injured at the interval. His first season with Rovers was climaxed by the resurrection of his international career as he went to Australia for a third time, this time with the Welsh World Championship team.

The following season Rovers again reached the final of the Yorkshire Cup and Clive got onto the score sheet but Leeds proved too strong with a 15-11 triumph on their own ground. In 1976-77 Rovers fought their way through to the semi-final of the Challenge Cup and after almost 16 years in the game Sully thought his moment had come. Sullivan scored a magical try after a thirty yard burst by Phil Lowe had set him free on the "25" but Widnes proved too tough, winning 14-5. It looked as if Sullivan would never win that most coveted of medals. Still Rovers continued to win things. In 1977-78 it was the Floodlit Trophy with Clive grabbing a superlative touch-down in the 26-11 pasting of St. Helens and in 1978-79 the First Division Championship went to Craven Park. When Sully scored against Huddersfield at Craven Park on April 13th, 1979 he became the only man to have registered a century of tries for both Hull and Rovers. The previous October had been notable in that for the first time Sullivan appeared on his native soil in a first-class match when he

Clive Sullivan introduces Phil Lowe to French officials prior to a
Test Match at Toulouse in 1972.

took the field at Swansea for Wales against Australia at the age of 35.

Season 1979-80 was to be Clive's swan-song with Hull Kingston and what a year it proved to be. In December he found himself lining up against his old club at the Boulevard which was bursting at the seams for the occasion was the Final of the Floodlit Trophy. Sully would have had mixed feelings that night as Hull won 13-3. There was no doubt about his feelings on March 22nd, 1980, however, for that was the day that Hull K.R. defeated Halifax 20-7 at Headingley in the semi-final of the Challenge Cup to fulfil a dream. Appropriately enough, Clive scored twice, and, although it was not known at the time, his second try was the 400th of his career. To complete his fairy tale Rovers' opponents at Wembley were to be Hull. (Sullivan had appeared at Wembley in 1973 in a test against Australia).

The Empire Stadium was filled to capacity for this Humberside derby of derbies. It was Sullivan's 600th appearance (plus one substitution) in first-class Rugby League and it was to be his finale with Rovers. The game never lived up to expectations but Clive at last got his hands on that winners' medal as Hull went down 10-5. It had been a long, hard road but Sullivan had still not got to the end of it. He surprised many by joining Oldham for the 1980-81 campaign, scoring on his debut at Swinton but having his season terminated by a fractured arm.

By August 1981 the wheel of fortune had turned full circle for Clive who rejoined Hull as "A" team coach. He was occasionally called upon to assist in the first team but could hardly be expected to win a Challenge Cup with the club he had joined almost 21 years before. Hull were a powerful, personality-packed team when Sully arrived at the Boulevard the second time around and he did not figure prominently, if at all, in their overall first team strategy. The black and whites duly reached Wembley in 1982 where they fought out an anti-climatic draw with cup kings Widnes. The replay was held at Elland Road, Leeds and Sullivan was drafted into the side when New Zealand test winger, Dane O'Hara pulled out injured. A full house saw a much more entertaining affair than Wembley had housed and Sully was rewarded with a second winners' medal as Hull finished on the right side of an 18-9 score-line. To win two Challenge Cup medals within three years after waiting nearly nineteen was, as they say, something else.

In 1982-83 Clive left Hull to become coach at Doncaster and for two seasons toiled to lift the Cinderella club of League off the bottom continuing to turn out occasionally as a player although then past his 40th birthday.

Tatters Field, Doncaster was a far cry from some of the stadia across the Rugby League playing world in which Sullivan scintillated at international and test level for there is no denying that Clive was one of the sport's greatest at that rarified level. His first step on the ladder to international stardom was trodden when he played for the Under-24 team against France at Bayonne in November 1966. Two months later he won the first of seventeen test caps when he filled the left wing berth against the French at Carcassonne. Sullivan did not have a particularly good match but still contrived to score two tries. His second, in fact, won the match for Britain were down 11-13 with five minutes remaining when Sullivan was served inside his own half and went through the French for a sensational try which had 15,000 Frenchmen in raptures. Thirteen Britons was passably pleased too. Selection for Great Britain's World Cup squad for Australasia in 1968 followed and although the British were thoroughly disappointing, Clive certainly was not. He appeared in all three World Cup matches and bagged four tries, including a hat-trick as Britain beat New Zealand at Sydney. Seven more tries in three up-country games had the Aussies drooling and they expected miracles from him when he returned with the 1970 Great Britain tourists. Unfortunately he only played one test and the Aussies were deprived of seeing him at his best as niggling injuries took their toll. He was back for the whole of the home series against New Zealand in 1971-72 and the same season was appointed captain for the two tests against France, scoring tries in both.

Sullivan is best remembered for his wonderful performances as skipper of the Great Britain team which lifted the World Cup in France in 1972. Sully grabbed a try in each of Britain's four matches, thus equalling Johnny Thomas' feat of scoring in six successive tests. Of course, everyone remembers the magnificent effort he produced in the Final at Lyons when Britain clinched the cup by holding the Australians to a breathtaking 10-10 draw. His length of the field try will be talked about for as long as the game endures but it did not win the tournament for after it was scored the Kangaroos stormed back to lead 10-5. Sullivan, however, had not finished and backed up a mid-field break by Phil Lowe seven minutes from time. A lovely swerving run pierced the Australian defence before Sullivan linked with Brian Lockwood who put hooker Mick Stephenson over for the equalising try.

Three tests against the 1973 Kangaroos rounded off Sully's test career which brought him 13 tries and the captaincy on nine occasions. His career for Wales extended over the period 1968-1979 and encompassed 15 caps and seven tries. In view of his marked success as captain of the test team it is surprising that he was never accorded the captaincy of Wales, serving at various times under John Mantle, Gordon Lewis, David Watkins and Bill Francis.

Only two Welshmen have scored more tries than Clive Sullivan and only half-a-dozen players of any nationality have emulated him in topping 400 touchdowns. For that reason alone he will always rank among the great finishers. None of the others, however, had faced so many obstacles in their quest for glory.

CLIVE SULLIVAN'S PLAYING RECORD FOR HULL

	GAMES	TRIES	GOALS	POINTS
1961-62	17	13	—	39
1962-63	8	6	—	18
1963-64	7	7	—	21
1964-65	27	18	—	54
1965-66	37	23	—	69
1966-67	28	28	—	84
1967-68	20	17	—	51
1968-69	17	12	—	36
1969-70	39	21	—	63
1970-71	41	33	—	99
1971-72	40	30	—	90
1972-73	29	18	—	54
1973-74	30	21	—	63
1981-82	5+4 subs	1	—	3
1982-83	2	2	—	6
1984-85	0+1subs	—	—	—
TOTALS	347+5 subs	250	—	750

CLIVE SULLIVAN'S PLAYING RECORD FOR HULL K.R.

	GAMES	TRIES	GOALS	POINTS
1974-75	30	28	—	84
1975-76	40	16	—	48
1976-77	36	21	—	63
1977-78	36	15	—	45
1978-79	34	21	—	63
1979-80	37	17	—	51
TOTALS	213	118	—	454

All first-class matches:

	GAMES	TRIES	GOALS	POINTS
	629+10subs	406	—	1,218

John Bevan
(Cardiff RU, Warrington RL)

Like Maurice Richards, John Charles Bevan was a true son of the
Rhondda – born on October 28th, 1950 at Llwynypia, raised in Tylorst-
own and educated at Ferndale Grammar School. Bevan followed remarkably closely in the footsteps of Richards, winning Schoolboy caps,
filling Maurice's boots on the left-wing for Cardiff before winning full
Welsh caps and touring with the British Lions. The pair were magnificent
wings under both codes but their styles could hardly have been more
different.

Richards, with that touch of elegance, almost sartorial (as far as
rugby togs would allow), undemonstrative and somehow perpetually
unhurried, was the very antithesis of John Bevan. Sleeves rolled up, socks
down to his ankles, Bevan looked more like one of the Bash Street Kids
and caused mayhem wherever he went. Muscular, bursting with power
and energy, Bevan simply epitomised aggression and determination and
he could not hide his joy when scoring tries. His clenched fist salute to the
crowds after he had done one of his demolition jobs on the opposition
never went down well with non-Wire fans but the Wilderspool faithful
rejoiced with him.

Bevan with the ball twenty yards out may be described as something
akin to a bellicose buffalo and if any winger faced with a packed defence
could make the line it was Bevan. John Bevan, all-action mean-machine,
was the man for that situation for he appeared completely fearless
whatever the odds. A six-footer with over thirteen stones to throw at
opponents and a very high weight-speed ratio, Bevan did not always
have to rely on strength. He was quite capable of showing a clean pair of
heels to opponents from his own half and if he could go round them
instead of through or over them he sometimes would. Many of his tries
were scored by sheer dogged persistence and there was no more dangerous winger with the ball at his feet. How many times did he chase
apparently wasted kicks to harry opponents into errors before scoring an
highly improbable try? It was just not possible to relax when faced with
the bustling Bevan for mistakes usually proved fatal.

As a Union player John Bevan had a spectacular if relatively short
career. Although a winger, he won three caps for Wales 15 Group as a
number 8 forward and five caps in his accustomed position for Wales 19
Group before joining the Cardiff club for the 1969-70 season. His appearances for Cardiff over four years were restricted to 35 during which he
scored 25 tries and most of his rugby was played with Cardiff College of
Education. Within three months of his twentieth birthday Bevan won his
first cap for Wales against England at the Arms Park. Wales won 22-6 and
Bevan celebrated with a try engineered by Barry John. The Welsh went
on to win their first Grand Slam since 1952 with John firmly entrenched

John Bevan disposes of Keith Fielding to score.
David Watkins in left background.
(Courtesy "The Rugby Leaguer")

in the left wing berth in all their triumphs. His talents were rewarded with selection for the 1971 Lions tour of New Zealand where he scored 17 tries to equal the record set by the great Irish winger, Tony O'Reilly. Bevan wreaked havoc on Kiwi defences with his powerhouse displays in the early part of the tour and played in the first test victory over the All Blacks at Dunedin but his form tailed off and David Duckham took his test spot.

Bevan won the last of his ten Welsh caps in 1973 when Wales went down 10-9 to the Scots at Murrayfield. Three months earlier in November 1972 that would have seemed an impossibility as he had agreed terms with Wigan. He was reported to have received a cheque for £12,000 and guarantees of at least £1,300 per season. At the eleventh hour, however, John decided to retain his amateur status and returned Wigan's cheque. Just how the Rugby Union authorities managed to turn a blind eye to this flirtation with professionalism remains a mystery for other players have down the years been ostracised for lighter degrees of dalliance with League.

His conversion to League was only a matter of procrastination, however, for it was to Wigan's traditional rivals, Warrington, that Bevan took his highly prized skills in September 1973, for an undisclosed fee. The Wire, under Alec Murphy, were set to become a major power in the game and Bevan joined them at a most opportune time. His introduction to the game in a home clash against Castleford on September 23rd was certainly an encounter to remember. After 28 minutes he had won the crowd's approval after smashing his way to a try from twenty yards out taking three defenders over with him. A repeat performance in the second half was thwarted when he was unceremoniously dumped over the touch-line at the corner-flag and he ended up having his ribs X-rayed at the local hospital. For good measure three players, including Murphy, were sent off. Quite a debut.!

All wingers arriving at Wilderspool are cursed for they can never hope to satisfy Wire fans who were privileged to witness the fantastic feats of the greatest winger who ever laced a boot, the balding, boney, ballet-footed Brian Bevan. Bearing the same surname as the Aussie maestro, John Bevan was doubly cursed but his dreadnought performances carved out for him his own place in Warrington's Valhalla. Bevan turned out to be a worthy successor to an illustrious line of Wilderspool wingers which numbers among its *allumni* Jack Fish, Tom Blinkhorn, Albert Johnson, Stan McCormick, Terry O'Grady and Brian Glover. There was too a strong tradition of Welsh flyers on the Warrington flanks. Pre-war years had seen the likes of Griff Jenkins, Steve Ray and Islwyn Davies parading their skills before the Wilderspool devotees. Ray had set a club record by bagging 33 tries in 1932-33 only to see Izzy Davies top it with 36 in 1938-39. Such totals became academic, however, when Brian Bevan arrived on the scene. In the post-war period Stan Powell, Roy

Francis, Roy Lambert and latterly Dennis Curling and Phil Ford have maintained the Welsh presence on the Warrington wings.

John Bevan thus found he had a lot to live up to and there can be no doubting that he did.

His first season in the game was one of uninterrupted success. In January, 1974 Bevan appeared in Warrington's hard earned 4-0 victory over Featherstone in the Final of the Captain Morgan Trophy and a fortnight later scored a stunning 40 yard try as the John Player Trophy was lifted with a 27-16 triumph over gallant Rochdale Hornets at Wigan. The last game of the season saw Wire take the Club Championship with a 13-12 verdict over Kel Coslett's St. Helens to furnish the novice winger with his fourth winners' medal in a career only eight months old. The third and most prized had been won the previous week when in his 34th professional game he had stepped out at Wembley in the Challenge Cup Final against Featherstone Rovers, the holders. A ferociously fought encounter ensued in which John saw precious little of the ball but that hardly mattered as Warrington took the cup for the first time in twenty years with a 24-9 victory.

The season was rounded off by Bevan's inclusion in the Great Britain squad to tour Australia and New Zealand during which his forceful, penetrative play yielded him 15 tries in 17 outings. He appeared in the first and third tests against Australia only for Britain to be beaten narrowly on both occasions. A try in the first New Zealand test could not prevent a 13-8 defeat but two tries in the third Kiwi test, when Britain took the series with a 20-0 whitewash, confirmed Bevan's lofty status with those New Zealanders who had witnessed his great feats as a Union Lion three years earlier. There were only to be two more test matches for Bevan as a League player as he scored tries in the first and third tests against Bobby Fulton's 1978 Kangaroos. In the first test at Wigan Bevan's power and determination were never better illustrated than when he capitalised on an Australian passing break-down at half-way, hacked on twice and in a synchronised dive with Graham "Wombat" Eadie, the Aussie's 15 stones full-back, got the touchdown. It appeared to be the match-winner for it gave Britain a 9-7 lead with less than 15 minutes remaining but the Aussies struck back hard to win 15-9. After missing the second test through a calf injury he was recalled for the deciding match at Headingley as a centre. The Australians won easily 23-6 to take the Ashes and Bevan's half-dozen tests had seen him on the winning side only once, yet he had contrived to claim five tries. There was no doubt that he was one man who had troubled the all-conquering Kangaroos. In 1979 he was selected to tour Australia once more but had to withdraw through injury, his place going to St. Helens' ex-Llanelli winger, Roy Mathias, a Welsh RU cap in 1970 against France.

Bevan was also selected for the Welsh team to tour down-under in the 1975 World Championship, but like Maurice Richards withdrew for

John Bevan racing past a French defender.

(Courtesy "The Rugby Leaguer")

family reasons. Bevan's contribution to the Welsh RL international sides was considerable, however. Capped 17 times beginning with a two try debut against the French at Swansea in 1975, he represented his country as a winger, centre and second-row forward and had the honour of captaining the side on four occasions. His appearances for Wales brought him five tries.

At club level Bevan and Warrington continued to win pots. In his second season Warrington almost won the floodlit Trophy but were thwarted by Salford who won a replay at Wilderspool 10-5 with Bevan scoring the Wire's only try. Warrington also progressed to the Challenge Cup Final thanks to a clinical display of finishing power by Bevan who scored a hat-trick in the 11-4 defeat of mighty Leeds in the semi-final. No other hat-tricks of tries have been achieved at the semi-final stage since the last war. Warrington were red-hot favourites to retain the Cup at the expense of local rivals Widnes. It must have seemed like Christmas to Bevan when he touched down after only five minutes from a fortuitous bounce of the ball following a planned move between prop Dave Chisnall and hooker Kevin Ashcroft which did not go exactly to plan but achieved the desired result. Widnes did not hand out any more presents and ran out winners 14-7 so Bevan had to be content with a runners-up medal. In 1980 and 1982 John figured at centre in Warrington's Lancashire Cup winning sides. In 1978 he scored the only try of the Players Trophy Final as Warrington beat Widnes 9-4 and in the Final of the same competition in 1981 Bevan claimed both tries as Barrow were vanquished 12-5. Warrington's success in cup football never really translated to league warfare, however, and the nearest the men in primrose and blue came to taking the First Division title was to finish second in 1978-79 and 1980-81.

On April 3rd, 1981 Bevan registered the 200th try of his Rugby League career as Warrington slammed Hull 38-3 at Wilderspool. By this stage Bevan was established as a centre, a position ideally suited to a player of his percussive power. It is as a flamboyant, flying winger, however, that the world of rugby will remember John Bevan, the Tylerstown Terror.

JOHN BEVAN'S PLAYING RECORD FOR WARRINGTON

	GAMES	TRIES	GOALS	POINTS
1973-74	35	22	—	66
1974-75	37	29	6	99
1975-76	31	18	—	54
1976-77	23	17	—	51
1977-78	39	30	—	90
1978-79	23	17	—	51
1979-80	34	25	—	75
1980-81	38	19	1dg	58
1981-82	28	5	—	15
1982-83	14	7	—	21
1983-84	19+1sub	10	—	40
1984-85	8	2	—	8
1985-86	2	—	—	—
TOTALS	331+1sub	201	7	628

All first-class matches:

	GAMES	TRIES	GOALS	POINTS
	368+2subs	224	7	697

Appendix I

Leading Welsh Scorers 1895 to date

	TRIES			GOALS	
1895-96	F.W. Cooper (Bradford)	9	F.W. Cooper (Bradford)		33
1896-97	F.W. Cooper (Bradford)	10	F.W. Cooper (Bradford)		24
1897-98	J. Hoskins (Salford)	30	F.W. Cooper (Bradford)		36
1898-99	T.D. Davies (Oldham)	31	F.W. Cooper (Bradford)		40
1899-1900	T.D. Davies (Oldham)	27	F.W. Cooper (Bradford)		38
1900-01	L.I. Deere (Huddersfield)	28	W.P. Davies (Batley)		37
1901-02	T.D. Davies (Leeds)	19	W. James (Broughton R.)		75
1902-03	W.Evans (Leeds)	27	W.P. Davies (Batley)		47
1903-04	L.I. Deere (Huddersfield)	13	W.P. Davies (Batley)		19
	W. Thomas (Salford)	13			
1904-05	L.I. Deere (Huddersfield)	13	W.P. Davies (Batley)		20
1905-06	W.F. Jowett (Hull K.R.)	18	W.P. Davies (Batley)		43
	L. Parry (Hull)	18			
1906-07	D. Thomas (Dewsbury)	40	W.P. Davies (Batley)		52
1907-08	D. Thomas (Dews. & Halifax)	31	W.P. Davies (Batley)		54
1908-09	W.J. Williams (Halifax)	49	W.P. Davies (Batley)		53
1909-10	W.J. Williams (Halifax)	25	J. Thomas (Wigan)		50
1910-11	A.J. Francis (Hull)	27	T.H. Grey (Huddersfield)		47
1911-12	W.T. Davies (Halifax)	25	T.H. Grey (Huddersfield)		96
1912-13	W. Sandham (Hull K.R.)	25	J. Thomas (Wigan)		84
1913-14	W.H. Davies (Leeds)	22	J. Thomas (Wigan)		83
	T.B. Jenkins (Wigan)	22			
1914-15	J.H. Rogers (Huddersfield)	26	B. Gronow (Huddersfield)		140
1918-19	A.J. Francis (Hull)	25	J. Thomas (Wigan)		17
1919-20	A.J. Francis (Hull)	38	B. Gronow (Huddersfield)		148
1920-21	B. Williams (Batley)	21	B. Gronow (Huddersfield)		61
1921-22	J.A. Bacon (Leeds)	28	J. Sullivan (Wigan)		100
1922-23	J. Ring (Wigan)	41	J. Sullivan (Wigan)		161
1923-24	J. Ring (Wigan)	49	J. Sullivan (Wigan)		158
1924-25	J. Ring (Wigan)	54	J. Sullivan (Wigan)		138
1925-26	J. Ring (Wigan)	63	J. Sullivan (Wigan)		131
1926-27	J. Ring (Wigan)	49	J. Sullivan (Wigan)		148
1927-28	F. Evans (Swinton)	28	J.F. Thompson (Leeds)		106
1928-29	J. Ring (Wigan)	35	J. Sullivan (Wigan)		107
1929-30	J. Ring (Wigan)	27	J. F. Thompson (Leeds)		111
1930-31	J. Ring (Wigan)	33	J. Sullivan (Wigan)		133
1931-32	F.G. Smart (Wakefield T.)	30	J. Sullivan (Wigan)		117
1932-33	J.C. Morley (Wigan)	48	J. Sullivan (Wigan)		146
1933-34	J.C. Morley (Wigan)	43	J. Sullivan (Wigan)		194
1934-35	J.C. Morley (Wigan)	49	J. Sullivan (Wigan)		165
1935-36	W.H. Johnson (Huddersfield)	29	J. Sullivan (Wigan)		117
	J.C. Morley (Wigan)	29			
1936-37	D. Madden (Huddersfield)	32	J. Sullivan (Wigan)		117
1937-38	D. Madden (Huddersfield)	32	J. Sullivan (Wigan)		135
1938-39	I. Davies (Warrington)	36	J. Sullivan (Wigan)		124
1939-40	E. Walters (Bradford N.)	25	J. Sullivan (Wigan)		66
1940-41	E. Walters (Bradford N.)	32	J. Sullivan (Wigan)		40
1941-42	R.L. Francis (Dewsbury)	29	J. Sullivan (Wigan)		49

Appendix I (continued)

	TRIES			GOALS	
1942-43	A.S. Edwards (Dewsbury)	19	J. Sullivan (Wigan)		49
1943-44	A.S. Edwards (Dewsbury)	19	W.T. Davies (Huddersfield)		47
1944-45	M.A. Meek (Halifax)	13	S. Powell (St. Helens)		20
			A.J. Risman (Dewsbury)		20
1945-46	G. Price (Leeds)	23	S. Powell (St. Helens & Broughton R.)		57
1946-47	E. Walters (Bradford N.)	34	S. Powell (Belle Vue Rangers)		62
1947-48	A.S. Edwards (Bradford N.)	36	E.H. Ward (Wigan)		141
1948-49	A.S. Edwards (Bradford N.)	23	E.H. Ward (Wigan)		155
	S. Llewellyn (St. Helens)	23			
1949-50	A.H. Daniels (Halifax)	36	A.J. Risman (Workington T.)		104
1950-51	S. Llewellyn (St. Helens)	26	A.J. Risman (Workington T.)		108
1951-52	A.H. Daniels (Halifax)	30	T. Griffiths (Doncaster)		89
1952-53	D.R. Bevan (Wigan)	40	T. Griffiths (Doncaster & Halifax)		117
1953-54	S. Llewellyn (St. Helens)	37	A.J. Risman (Workington T.)		138
1954-55	M. Davies (Leigh)	34	B.L. Jones (Leeds)		104
1955-56	W.J. Boston (Wigan)	49	T. Griffiths (Halifax)		147
1956-57	W.J. Boston (Wigan)	60	B.L. Jones (Leeds)		194
1957-58	M. Davies (Bradford N.)	45	B.L. Jones (Leeds)		139
1958-59	W.J. Boston (Wigan)	54	B.L. Jones (Leeds)		126
1959-60	W.J. Boston (Wigan)	47	G.D. Owen (Halifax)		145
1960-61	W.J. Boston (Wigan)	37	G.D. Owen (Halifax)		130
1961-62	W.J. Boston (Wigan)	51	B.L. Jones (Leeds)		117
1962-63	R. Glastonbury (Workington)	41	K. Coslett (St. Helens)		156
1963-64	W.J. Boston (Wigan)	26	K. Coslett (St. Helens)		138
1964-65	J. Freeman (Halifax)	28	R. James (Halifax)		125
1965-66	C.A. Sullivan (Hull)	23	R. James (Halifax)		92
1966-67	C.A. Sullivan (Hull)	30	R. James (Halifax)		85
1967-68	T.B. Jones (Bradford N.)	26	T.G. Price (Bradford N.)		97
1968-69	F.H. Wilson (St. Helens)	24	K. Coslett (St. Helens)		158
1969-70	F.H. Wilson (St. Helens)	36	K. Coslett (St. Helens)		161
1970-71	C.A. Sullivan (Hull)	33	K. Coslett (St. Helens)		193
1971-72	M.C.R. Richards (Salford)	35	K. Coslett (St. Helens)		214
1972-73	M.C.R. Richards (Salford)	38	D. Watkins (Salford)		221
1973-74	R. Mathias (St. Helens)	40	D. Watkins (Salford)		183
1974-75	J.C. Bevan (Warrington)	31	K. Coslett (St. Helens)		129
1975-76	M.C.R. Richards (Salford)	37	D. Watkins (Salford)		175
1976-77	R. Mathias (St. Helens)	23	D. Watkins (Salford)		125
	M.C.R. Richards (Salford)	23			
1977-78	J.C. Bevan (Warrington)	30	P. Woods (Widnes)		122
1978-79	P. Prendiville (Hull)	25	P. Woods (Widnes & Rochdale H.)		46
1979-80	R. Mathias (St. Helens)	27	S. Diamond (Wakefield T.)		116
1980-81	J. C. Bevan (Warrington)	19	S. Diamond (Wakefield T.)		112
1981-82	L. Hopkins (Workington T.)	23	L. Hopkins (Workington T.)		190
1982-83	T. David (Cardiff City)	26	S. Diamond (Fulham)		136
1983-84	T. David (Cardiff City)	22	L. Hallett (Cardiff City)		140*
	D.J. Wilson (Swinton)	22			
1984-85	P. Ford (Warrington & Wigan)	19	C. Griffiths (Salford)		118
1985-86	P. Ford (Wigan & Bradford N.)	17	C. Griffiths (Salford)		39
1986-87	P. Ford (Bradford N.)	30	G. Pearce (Hull)		53
			P. Prendiville (York)		53

*Hallett's total included 29 drop goals –
the highest since the one-point drop goal
was introduced in 1974-75.

172

Appendix II

Scoring in a Season – Progressive Records by Welsh Players

TRIES

9	by Fred (F.W.) Cooper	1895-96	for Bradford
10	by Fred (F.W.) Cooper	1896-97	for Bradford
*30	by Joe Hoskins	1897-98	for Salford
31	by Tom (T.D.) Davies	1898-99	for Oldham
40	by Dai Thomas	1906-07	for Dewsbury
*49	by Billy (W.J.) Williams	1908-09	for Halifax
49	by Johnny Ring	1923-24	for Wigan
54	by Johnny Ring	1924-25	for Wigan
63	by Johnny Ring	1925-26	for Wigan

GOALS

33	by Fred (F.W.) Cooper	1895-96	for Bradford
36	by Fred (F.W.) Cooper	1897-98	for Bradford
40	by Fred (F.W.) Cooper	1898-99	for Bradford
*75	by Willie James	1901-02	for Broughton Rangers
96	by Tommy (T.H.) Grey	1911-12	for Huddersfield
*140	by Ben Gronow	1914-15	for Huddersfield
*148	by Ben Gronow	1919-20	for Huddersfield
*161	by Jim Sullivan	1922-23	for Wigan
*194	by Jim Sullivan	1933-34	for Wigan
*194	by Lewis (B.L.) Jones	1956-57	for Leeds
214	by Kel Coslett	1971-72	for St. Helens
*221	by David Watkins	1972-73	for Salford

POINTS

104	by Fred (F.W.) Cooper	1895-96	for Bradford
107	by Tom Williams	1897-98	for Salford
120	by Wattie (W.P.) Davies	1898-99	for Batley
159	by Willie James	1901-02	for Broughton Rangers
219	by Tommy (T.H.) Grey	1911-12	for Huddersfield
*292	by Ben Gronow	1914-15	for Huddersfield
*332	by Ben Gronow	1919-20	for Huddersfield
*349	by Jim Sullivan	1922-23	for Wigan
*406	by Jim Sullivan	1933-34	for Wigan
*496	by Lewis (B.L.) Jones	1956-57	for Leeds

* Denotes that these totals were also all-time Rugby League records at the time.
The goals kicked by David Watkins in 1972-73 and the points scored by Lewis Jones in 1956-57 remain Rugby League records to this day.

Appendix III

Welsh Players who have topped the League's Scoring Lists

TRIES

1897-98	Joe Hoskins (Salford)	30
1902-03	W. Evans (Leeds)	27
1908-09	W.J. Williams (Halifax)	49
	(Williams tied for top place with Wigan winger Joe Miller)	
1918-19	Alf (A.J.) Francis (Hull)	25
1922-23	Johnny Ring (Wigan)	41
1923-24	Johnny Ring (Wigan)	49
1924-25	Johnny Ring (Wigan)	54
1925-26	Johnny Ring (Wigan)	63
1934-35	Jack Morley (Wigan)	49
1940-41	Emlyn Walters (Bradford Northern)	32
1941-42	Roy (R.L.) Francis (Dewsbury)	29
1956-57	Billy (W.J.) Boston (Wigan)	60
1961-62	Billy (W.J.) Boston (Wigan)	51
1962-63	Ray Glastonbury (Workington Town)	41
1975-76	Maurice (M.C.R.) Richards (Salford)	37

GOALS

1899-1900	Fred (F.W.) Cooper (Bradford)	39
1901-02	Willie James (Broughton Rangers)	75
1914-15	Ben Gronow (Huddersfield)	140
1919-20	Ben Gronow (Huddersfield)	148
1921-22	Jim Sullivan (Wigan)	100
1922-23	Jim Sullivan (Wigan)	161
1923-24	Jim Sullivan (Wigan)	158
1924-25	Jim Sullivan (Wigan)	138
1925-26	Jim Sullivan (Wigan)	131
1926-27	Jim Sullivan (Wigan)	148
1927-28	Joe Thompson (Leeds)	106
1928-29	Jim Sullivan (Wigan)	107
1929-30	Joe Thompson (Leeds)	111
1930-31	Jim Sullivan (Wigan)	133
1931-32	Jim Sullivan (Wigan)	117
1932-33	Jim Sullivan (Wigan)	146
1933-34	Jim Sullivan (Wigan)	194
1934-35	Jim Sullivan (Wigan)	165
1935-36	Jim Sullivan (Wigan)	117
1936-37	Jim Sullivan (Wigan)	117
1937-38	Jim Sullivan (Wigan)	135
1938-39	Jim Sullivan (Wigan)	124
1947-48	Ted (E.H.) Ward (Wigan)	141
1948-49	Ted (E.H.) Ward (Wigan)	155
1956-57	Lewis (B.L.) Jones (Leeds)	194

1962-63	Kel Coslett (St. Helens)	156
1963-64	Kel Coslett (St. Helens)	138
1970-71	Kel Coslett (St. Helens)	193
1971-72	Kel Coslett (St. Helens)	214
1972-73	David Watkins (Salford)	221
1973-74	David Watkins (Salford)	183
1975-76	David Watkins (Salford)	175
1981-82	Lynn Hopkins (Workington Town)	190
1982-83	Steve Diamond (Fulham)	136

POINTS

1902-03	Wattie (W.P.) Davies (Batley)	136
1912-13	Johnny Thomas (Wigan)	198
1914-15	Ben Gronow (Huddersfield)	292
1919-20	Ben Gronow (Huddersfield)	332
1922-23	Jim Sullivan (Wigan)	349
1923-24	Jim Sullivan (Wigan)	319
1924-25	Jim Sullivan (Wigan)	288
1925-26	Jim Sullivan (Wigan)	274
1926-27	Jim Sullivan (Wigan)	320
1927-28	Joe Thompson (Leeds)	233
1928-29	Jim Sullivan (Wigan)	226
1929-30	Joe Thompson (Leeds)	243
1930-31	Jim Sullivan (Wigan)	278
1931-32	Jim Sullivan (Wigan)	249
1932-33	Jim Sullivan (Wigan)	307
1933-34	Jim Sullivan (Wigan)	406
1934-35	Jim Sullivan (Wigan)	348
1935-36	Jim Sullivan (Wigan)	246
1937-38	Jim Sullivan (Wigan)	285
1938-39	Gus (A.J.) Risman (Salford)	267
1947-48	Ted (E.H.) Ward (Wigan)	312
1948-49	Ted (E.H.) Ward (Wigan)	361
1956-57	Lewis (B.L.) Jones (Leeds)	496
1962-63	Kel Coslett (St. Helens)	321
1970-71	Kel Coslett (St. Helens)	395
1971-72	David Watkins (Salford)	473
1972-73	David Watkins (Salford)	493
1973-74	David Watkins (Salford)	438
1975-76	David Watkins (Salford)	385
1981-82	Lynn Hopkins (Workington Town)	446
1982-83	Steve Diamond (Fulham)	302

Appendix IV

Most Tries in a Match by Welsh Players

8	Dai Thomas	Dewsbury v Liverpool City	13th April, 1907
7	Johnny Ring	Wigan v Flimby & Fothergill (Cup)	14th February, 1925
7	Johnny Ring	Wigan v Salford	13th April, 1925
7	Johnny Ring	Wigan v Pemberton Rovers (Cup)	12th February, 1927
7	Billy Boston	Wigan v Dewsbury	20th August, 1955
7	Billy Boston	Wigan v Salford	30th April, 1962
7	Clive Sullivan	Hull v Doncaster	15th April, 1968
6	Billy (W.J.) Williams	Halifax v Keighley	1st January, 1909
6	Will (W.T.) Davies	Halifax v York (Cup)	18th February, 1911
6	Bill Sandham	Hull K.R. v Coventry	1st March, 1913
6	Alf Francis	Hull v B.O.C.M. (Cup)	21st February, 1920
6	Johnny Ring	Wigan v Wigan Highfield	13th January, 1923
6	Johnny Ring	Wigan v Rochdale Hornets	25th December, 1930
6	Trevor Foster	Bradford N. v Wakefield Trinity	10th April, 1948
6	Billy Boston	Great Britain v Northern N.S.W.	7th July, 1954
6	Stuart Llewellyn	St. Helens v Castleford	3rd March, 1956
6	Stuart Llewellyn	St. Helens v Liverpool City	20th August, 1956
6	Billy Boston	Wigan v Widnes	2nd April, 1960
6	Billy Boston	Wigan v Dewsbury	9th April, 1960

** All the above players were wing-three-quarters with the exception of Trevor Foster and Bill Sandham who scored their tries from the pack.

** Dai Thomas' eight tries has only been bettered on three occasions..

Most Goals in a Match by Welsh Players

22	Jim Sullivan	Wigan v Flimby & Fothergill (Cup)	14th February, 1925
15	Lewis Jones	Great Britain v Southern N.S.W.	21st August. 1954
13	George Lewis	St. Helens v Wardley (Cup)	16th February, 1924
13	Gus Risman	Salford v Bramley	5th April, 1933
13	Gus Risman	Salford v Broughton Rangers	18th May, 1940
13	Jim Sullivan	Wigan v Batley	23rd January, 1943
13	Lewis Jones	Leeds v Blackpool Borough	19th August, 1957
13	David Watkins	Salford v Keighley	7th January, 1972

** Jim Sullivan's 22 goals is the highest ever recorded in first-class Rugby League.

Most Points in a Match by Welsh Players

44	Jim Sullivan	as above	14th February, 1925
33	George Thomas	Warrington v St. Helens	12th April, 1909
32	Gus Risman	Salford v Bramley	5th April, 1933
32	Gus Risman	Salford v Broughton Rangers	18th May, 1940
31	Lewis Jones	Leeds v Bradford Northern	22nd August, 1956
30	Lewis Jones	Great Britain v Southern N.S.W.	21st August, 1954
30	Lynn Hopkins	Workington Town v Doncaster	4th April, 1982

** Only "Tich" West (Hull K.R.) with 53 points in a game against Brookland Rovers in 1905 has exceeded Sullivan's 44 points in a match.

Appendix V

Highest Seasonal Scoring Feats by Welsh Players

TRIES IN A SEASON		GOALS IN A SEASON	
*63	Johnny Ring (Wigan), 1925-6	*221	David Watkins (Salford), 1972-73
60	Billy Boston (Wigan), 1956-57	214	Kel Coslett (St. Helens), 1971-72
54	Johnny Ring (Wigan), 1924-25	194	Jim Sullivan (Wigan), 1933-34
54	Billy Boston (Wigan), 1958-59	194	Lewis Jones (Leeds), 1956-57
51	Billy Boston (Wigan), 1961-62	193	Kel Coslett (St. Helens), 1970-71
49	Billy Williams (Halifax), 1908-09	193	David Watkins (Salford), 1971-72
49	Johnny Ring (Wigan), 1923-24	190	Lynn Hopkins (Workington Town), 1981-82
49	Johnny Ring (Wigan), 1926-27	183	David Watkins (Salford), 1973-74
49	Jack Morley (Wigan), 1934-35	175	David Watkins (Salford), 1975-76
48	Billy Boston (Wigan), 1955-56	166	Stuart Ferguson (Leigh), 1970-71
48	Johnny Freeman (Halifax), 1956-57	165	Jim Sullivan (Wigan), 1934-35
47	Billy Boston (Wigan), 1959-60	162	Kel Coslett (St. Helens), 1972-73
45	Malcolm Davies (Bradford N.), 1957-58	161	Jim Sullivan (Wigan), 1922-23
43	Jack Morley (Wigan), 1933-34	161	Kel Coslett (St. Helens), 1969-70
43	Billy Boston (Wigan), 1957-58	158	Jim Sullivan (Wigan), 1923-24
41	Johnny Ring (Wigan), 1957-58	156	Kel Coslett (St. Helens), 1962-63
41	Ray Glastonbury (Workington T.), 1962-63	155	Ted Ward (Wigan), 1948-49
40	Dai Thomas (Dewsbury), 1906-07	155	David Watkins (Salford), 1970-71
40	Dai Bevan (Wigan), 1952-53	154	Kel Coslett (St. Helens), 1968-69
40	Roy Mathias (St. Helens), 1973-74	148	Ben Gronow (Huddersfield), 1919-20
38	Alf Francis (Hull), 1919-20	148	Jim Sullivan (Wigan), 1926-27
38	Stuart Llewellyn (St. Helens), 1955-56	147	Tyssul Griffiths (Halifax), 1955-56
38	Johnny Freeman (Halifax), 1957-58	146	Jim Sullivan (Wigan), 1932-33
37	Stuart Llewellyn (St. Helens), 1953-54	145	Garfield Owen (Halifax), 1959-60
37	Billy Boston (Wigan), 1960-61	143	Terry Price (Bradford N.), 1968-69
37	Maurice Richards (Salford), 1975-76	141	Ted Ward (Wigan), 1947-48
36	Izzy Davies (Warrington), 1938-39	140	Ben Gronow (Huddersfield), 1914-15
36	Alan Edwards (Bradford N.), 1947-48	140	Lyn Hallett (Cardiff City), 1983-84
36	Arthur Daniels (Halifax), 1949-50	139	Lewis Jones (Leeds), 1957-58
36	Lewis Jones (Leeds), 1956-57	138	Jim Sullivan (Wigan), 1924-25
36	Frank Wilson (St. Helens), 1969-70	138	Gus Risman (Workington Town), 1953-54
35	Dai Thomas (Halifax), 1908-09	138	Kel Coslett (St. Helens), 1963-64
35	Johnny Ring (Wigan), 1928-29	136	Steve Diamond (Fulham), 1982-83
35	Stuart Llewellyn (St. Helens), 1952-53	135	Jim Sullivan (Wigan), 1937-38
35	Maurice Richards (Salford), 1971-72	134	Kel Coslett (St. Helens), 1973-74
34	Alan Edwards (Salford), 1938-39	133	Jim Sullivan (Wigan), 1930-31
34	Emlyn Walters (Bradford N.), 1946-47	131	Jim Sullivan (Wigan), 1925-26
34	Malcolm Davies (Leigh), 1954-55	130	Garfield Owen (Halifax), 1960-61
34	Arthur Daniels (Halifax), 1955-56	129	Kel Coslett (St. Helens), 1974-75
		126	Lewis Jones (Leeds), 1958-59
		125	Ronnie James (Halifax), 1964-65
		125	David Watkins (Salford), 1976-77
		124	Jim Sullivan (Wigan), 1938-39
		124	Lewis Jones (Leeds), 1953-54
		123	Ronnie James (Halifax), 1962-63
		123	Garfield Owen (Keighley), 1962-63
		122	Paul Woods (Widnes), 1977-78

*Constitutes the most tries scored
by a British player: Ellery Hanley (Wigan)
equalled this record in 1986-87.

*Constitutes the World record.

Scorers of 300 points in a Season

*496	Lewis Jones (Leeds), 1956-57
493	David Watkins (Salford), 1972-73
476	David Watkins (Salford), 1971-72
452	Kel Coslett (St. Helens), 1971-72
446	Lynn Hopkins, (Workington Town), 1981-82
438	David Watkins (Salford), 1973-74
406	Jim Sullivan (Wigan), 1933-34
395	Kel Coslett (St. Helens), 1970-71
385	David Watkins, (Salford), 1975-76
361	Ted Ward (Wigan), 1948-49
358	David Watkins (Salford), 1970-71
356	Stuart Ferguson (Leigh), 1970-71
349	Jim Sullivan (Wigan), 1922-23
348	Jim Sullivan (Wigan), 1934-35
332	Ben Gronow (Huddersfield), 1919-20
330	Kel Coslett (St. Helens), 1972-73
325	Kel Coslett (St. Helens), 1969-70
321	Kel Coslett (St. Helens), 1962-63
320	Jim Sullivan (Wigan), 1926-27
320	Lewis Jones (Leeds), 1957-58
319	Jim Sullivan (Wigan), 1923-24
317	Kel Coslett (St. Helens), 1968-69
313	Terry Price (Bradford N.), 1968-69
312	Ted Ward (Wigan), 1947-48
307	Jim Sullivan (Wigan), 1932-33
302	Lewis Jones (Leeds), 1953-54
302	Steve Diamond (Fulham), 1982-83
302	Clive Griffiths (Salford), 1984-85
300	Lewis Jones (Leeds), 1958-59

*Constitutes the world record.

Appendix VI

Welshmen who have Scored 200 Tries

571	Billy Boston (1953-70) – Wigan, Blackpool Borough
418	Johnny Ring (1922-33) – Wigan, Rochdale Hornets
406	Clive Sullivan (1961-84) – Hull, Hull K.R., Oldham, Doncaster
302	Maurice Richards (1969-83) – Salford
294	Alan Edwards (1935-49) – Salford, Dewsbury, Bradford Northern
291	Johnny Freeman (1954-67) – Halifax
268	Arthur Daniels (1945-59) – Halifax, Bradford Northern
240	Stuart Llewellyn (1948-58) – St. Helens
240	Roy Mathias (1972-84) – St. Helens
238	Jack Morley (1932-39) – Wigan
232	Gus Risman (1929-54) – Salford, Dewsbury, Workington Town, Batley
229	Roy Francis (1937-55) – Wigan, Barrow, Dewsbury, Warrington, Hull
222	John Bevan (1973-84) – Warrington
220	Frank Evans (1921-31) – Swinton
220	Bert Jenkins (1904-20) – Wigan
215	Frank Wilson (1968-82) – St. Helens, Workington T., Warrington, Salford, Cardiff City

Welshmen who have Kicked 400 Goals

2,867	Jim Sullivan (1921-46) – Wigan
1,698	Kel Coslett (1962-79) – St. Helens, Rochdale Hornets
1,678	Gus Risman (1929-54) – Salford, Dewsbury, Workington Town, Batley
1,449	Lewis Jones (1952-64) – Leeds
1,342	David Watkins (1967-83) – Salford, Swinton, Cardiff City
1,030	Ron James (1961-71) – Halifax
921	Joe Thompson (1923-33) – Leeds
890	Garfield Owen (1956-65) – Halifax, Keighley
849	George Lewis (1922-36) – St. Helens
826	Ben Gronow (1910-29) – Huddersfield, Batley, Featherstone Rovers
761	Tuss Griffiths (1946-56) – Hunslet, Doncaster, Halifax, Dewsbury
719	Tommy Rees (1928-44) – Oldham, Broughton Rangers
661	Steve Diamond (1978-87) – Wakefield Trinity, Fulham, Warrington, Hunslet, Castleford, York
580	Ted Ward (1938-53) – Wigan, Cardiff, Oldham
495	Wattie Davies (1896-1912) – Batley
484	Johnny Thomas (1904-20) – Wigan
470	Jack Davies (1947-55) – Salford
442	Terry Price (1967-71) – Bradford Northern
441	Clive Griffiths (1979-86) – St. Helens, Salford
425	Lynn Hopkins (1979-84) – Workington Town, Kent Invicta

Welshmen who have Scored 1,000 Points

6,022   Jim Sullivan (1921-46) – Wigan
4,052   Gus Risman (1929-54) – Salford, Dewsbury, Workington Town, Batley
3,545   Kel Coslett (1962-79) – St. Helens, Rochdale Hornets
3,372   Lewis Jones (1952-64) – Leeds
3,117   David Watkins (1967-83) – Salford, Swinton, Cardiff City
2,195   Ron James (1961-71) – Halifax
2,043   Joe Thompson (1923-33) – Leeds
1,910   Ben Gronow (1910-29) – Huddersfield, Batley, Featherstone Rovers
1,836   George Lewis (1922-36) – St. Helens
1,801   Garfield Owen (1956-65) – Halifax, Keighley
1,727   Billy Boston (1953-70) – Wigan, Blackpool Borough
1,564   Tuss Griffiths (1946-56) – Hunslet, Doncaster, Halifax, Dewsbury
1,459   Tommy Rees (1928-44) – Oldham, Broughton Rangers
1,400   Wattie Davies (1896-1912) – Batley
1,368   Steve Diamond (1978-87) – Wakefield Trinity, Fulham, Hunslet, Warrington,
        Castleford, York
1,361   Ted Ward (1938-53) – Wigan, Cardiff, Oldham
1,328   Johnny Thomas (1904-20) – Wigan
1,260   Johnny Ring (1922-33) – Wigan, Rochdale Hornets
1,218   Clive Sullivan (1961-84) – Hull, Hull K.R., Oldham, Doncaster
1,090   Jack Davies (1947-55) – Salford
1,022   Alan Edwards (1935-49) – Salford, Dewsbury, Bradford Northern
1,012   Lynn Hopkins (1979-84) – Workington Town, Kent Invicta

Addenda & Errata to Volume I

Page 11   line 12 succeed should read excede
Page 45   Joe Jones transferred from Wigan to Barrow in 1944
Page 72   line 19 should read 1962, not 1963
Page 83   line 37 Davies' drop-goal was the last four-point drop-goal kicked by a Welshman in the international championship
Page 141   J. Thomas was captain of Wales on April 1st, 1911
Page 150   R. Wanbon (St. Helens) played at number 10 against France on October 23rd, 1969
Page 166   line 7 (272) should read (278)
Page 170   Benyon should read Beynon
Page 171   JONES David joined Merthyr Tydfil NU Club, not Treherbert NU
                 MOORE William J. joined Rochdale H., not Oldham
Page 172   TRUMP Robert should read TRUMP Leonard C.
Appendix VII   Detailed research now indicates that Jere Blake and William Morris appear never to have signed for Salford or any other professional club although they do appear to have trialled for Northern Union clubs.
                 To this list may now be added Rob Ackerman (to Whitehaven), Stuart Evans (to St. Helens) and Gary Pearce (to Hull)
Page 42   Further research into Jim Sullivan's monumental statistics indicates that in 1933-34 he played 37 times for Wigan scoring 6 tries, 159 goals, 336 points. In 1936-37 his appearances totalled 40 and in 1937-38 they totalled 37. His peace-time totals for Wigan should now read:
                     733 games   73 tries   2,213 goals   4,645 points
                 His record in all first-class matches should now read:
                     928 games   96 tries   2,867 goals   6,022 points

THREE FASCINATING BOOKS ON RUGBY LEAGUE BY ROBERT GATE

 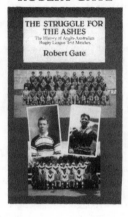 

"GONE NORTH" (Volume I)   £7.25 (softback)
The story of some of Wales' greatest Rugby League players. Features Billy Boston, Jim Sullivan, Wattie Davies, Trevor Foster, Roy Francis, John Mantle, Colin Dixon and many more.
> *"An unusual and compelling history"* – Paul Fitzpatrick, *"The Guardian"*
> *"A thoroughly readable book"* – John Kennedy, *"South Wales Echo"*
> *"Compelling reading for followers of both codes"* – Raymond Fletcher, *"Yorkshire Post"*

"THE STRUGGLE FOR THE ASHES"   £8.00 (Softback), £11.50 (Hardback)
Match by match accounts of every Anglo-Australian test match 1908-1984. Superbly illustrated.
> *"Not only a statistician's dream but a darned, good read"* – Brian Smith, Bradford *"Telegraph & Argus"*
> *"Quite simply the best book on Rugby League, ever"* – *"Leeds Other Paper"*
> *"One of the game's most ambitious writing projects has turned out a winner"* – David Middleton, *"Rugby League Week"*
> *"If points are awarded for this book, Mr. Gate scores ten out of ten"* – John Billot, *"The Western Mail"*

"CHAMPIONS"   £12.00 (Softback), £15.75 (Hardback)
A pictorial and statistical celebration of the Rugby League Championship 1895-1987.
> *"Nostalgia drips from the pages"* – Harry Edgar, *"Open Rugby"*
> *"The photographs alone were worth the price"* – Ray French, *"Rugby Leaguer"*
> *"Professionally researched and produced and deserves a place on the bookshelf of anyone with an eye for the history of the game"* – Phil Lyon, *"Halifax Evening Courier"*
> *"A Champion book in every respect"* – Raymond Fletcher, *"Yorkshire Post"*

ALL AVAILABLE FROM   R.E. GATE
                          FREEPOST (No stamp Required)
                          SOWERBY BRIDGE
                          WEST YORKSHIRE
                          HX6 4JP

Please make cheques payable to R.E. Gate
All prices include postage.